YOU CAN SELL
ANYTHING
BY TELEPHONE!

YOU CAN SELL ANYTHING BY TELEPHONE!

Dr. Gary S. Goodman

PRENTICE
HALL
PRESS

New York   London   Toronto   Sydney   Tokyo   Singapore

Prentice Hall Press
15 Columbus Circle
New York, New York 10023

Published in 1987 by Prentice Hall Press
A Division of Simon & Schuster, Inc.
Originally published by Prentice-Hall, Inc.

PRENTICE HALL PRESS is a trademark of Simon & Schuster Inc.

Library of Congress Cataloging-in-Publication Data

Goodman, Gary S.
You can sell anything by telephone!

Includes index.
1. Telephone selling.   I. Title.
HF5438.3.G67   1984   658.8′5   84-11579
ISBN 0-13-976762-2 (pbk.)

Manufactured in the United States of America

10   11   12   13   14

This book is dedicated to my wife, best friend, and colleague, Dr. Deanne Honeyman-Goodman, to the warm memories of my father, Bernard Goodman, and to Roy Honeyman.

CONTENTS

PREFACE

I sometimes think that I have come a long way after fifteen years in telemarketing and management. Then I stop to marvel at how far North American companies have come in the past fifteen months!

There has been a literal explosion of interest in telemarketing, spurred by the nationwide television campaigns waged by various telephone companies. We are all "reinventing" the telephone and its uses in the day-to-day affairs of the office and community.

You Can Sell Anything by Telephone! is your guide to profiting from our brave new world of telemarketing, where great fortunes are being made and redirected through the power of this medium. This book is geared to providing you with the most intelligent approach to the telemarketing process available anywhere. Through it, you will learn how to distinguish your message and yourself from those who are less polished and less professional.

This book builds upon my other recent volumes published by Prentice-Hall: *Winning by Telephone* (1982), *Reach Out & Sell Someone* (1983), and *Selling Skills for the Non-salesperson* (1984). If you have read these, I am sure you will find a substantial amount of new and useful information in

You Can Sell Anything by Telephone! If you are a stranger to these titles, I am confident you'll find this new book an appropriate introduction to my ideas.

I know you're going to like this book. Every idea has been tested across all major industries, and I can promise you that you'll be able to put these ideas to work right away.

You have my best wishes as you prove to yourself that *You Can Sell Anything by Telephone!*

YOU CAN SELL ANYTHING BY TELEPHONE!

CHAPTER ONE

FROM ROLLS-ROYCES TO PINK ELEPHANTS

What do automobiles, fine art prints, instant pictures, service agreements, and fine wines have in common? They can all be sold by telephone, as many companies are proving each and every day in major cities and small towns across North America.

It has been common knowledge that stockbrokers, travel agents, and insurance underwriters have always had to rely upon this tool for their leads, but today the phone is becoming an indispensable link to commercial power and success.

Item: Jules Pollack, an entrepreneur living in beautiful Carmel, California, and now president of Creative Balloons, used to fight the daily battle of making a living in Los Angeles before calamity struck. As he was walking up the driveway to his house, he saw his young son's skateboard and decided to give the device a flyer. As it turns out, it gave *him* a flyer, and he landed in the hospital for eight weeks. Several operations later, his ankle was sufficiently healed from its multiple breaks to permit him to return home.

No longer able to see people in person, as he did before by getting into the car and visiting various places of business, Jules reached out for the next best tool: the telephone. Reluctantly, he started closing business by phone, and he found, to his amazement and pleasure, that he could accomplish phenomenol things by phone. "It's the best thing that ever happened to me," Jules recalls. "We found that we didn't have to get on airplanes and drag ourselves across the country to open new business—all we had to do was get people on the phone! "

Jules saw another benefit in the phone—he could find one anywhere, and wherever he did, that's where his business was. He decided to move to "paradise," on the beautiful Monterey Peninsula, and the rest, as they say, is history.

BETTER THAN BEING THERE

Phone companies used to have a television commercial that said, "It's the next best thing to being there." This slightly defensive claim is too conservative, according to some researchers. In many cases, according to experts, the telephone is *better than being there.*

When we try to sell people while looking at them "eyeball to eyeball," several non-productive elements creep into the situation. Prejudice, for one. Prospects may not like us because we're too young or too old for their tastes, or because we wear our hair in a trendy manner, or because we drive a sports car, or because we wear comfortable shoes that don't sacrifice ease for fashion.

The proverbial first impressions that we hear so much about are really created by the *picture* someone receives from us. If they are looking at us, they will use their own usually narrow conceptions and stereotypes to judge us. Often, their first impressions, if negative, will yield to a more sensible image, but why should we go through the hassle if we don't have to?

By using the telephone, we are in the marvelous position of projecting the image we wish, unfettered by what we look like. As long as we can develop savvy strategies for constructing sales appeals and shaping our voices in subtle ways, we can do even better than we can in person.

Research tells us that difficult customers are often better handled by phone. For instance, instead of getting visibly agitated with them, as we could if we saw the steam coming from under their collars, we can concentrate upon what they are saying and come back with cool replies. Negotiation can be better done by phone, because we aren't giving ourselves and our positions away as we might inadvertantly do through eye contact and physical body language.

Selling, itself, can go much better by phone, for a number of reasons. In the current corporate world that we live in, selling takes on a "ritualistic" aspect. It appears as if things take a very long time to come to fruition. It may take us several visits to a site simply to determine whether we have a real, live prospect, or if we only have a "suspect," who isn't worth pursuing. We can waste our time wining and dining bozos who have no intention other than that of milking our company expense accounts.

By getting people on the phone, we find that we aren't constrained by the civilities that prevent us from asking frank questions in person. It's much easier to ask someone, "Do you have the authority to make a buying decision," which is a very pertinent question, over the phone than while we are in the person's presence. In person, we fear that we'll cause the prospect to lose face, so we tend to procrastinate and avoid bottom-line qualifying questions such as this.

Believe it or not, it's also easier to ask for big deals on the phone than it is in person. When we attach a great amount of ceremony to closing a deal, we make the matter seem very grave, and the buyer senses that there is a great deal of tension riding on his or her decision. When we ask for a yes or no by phone, it seems to be a much more simple matter, and we find that prospects are more inclined to take a plunge without the second-guessing that enters into sit-down meetings with us.

Recently, I spoke before a well-known breakfast club in Los Angeles on the subject of telemarketing, and my specific purpose was to inform the many businesspeople in the audience that they can accomplish great things by phone, if only they give themselves a chance. After the program, I received a call from a computer retailer who had heard my talk. He was bursting with enthusiasm as he told me that he tried closing a prospect over the phone instead of attempting this in person.

"I simply assumed that we were going to do business," he

said, echoing the mood he picked up from my speech. "I said, 'What we'll do is put you down for one of our personal models,' and he said, 'Why not?' "

I asked the fellow why he hadn't tried to close over the phone before, and he said, "I didn't think you could!"

TELEMARKETING ISN'T NEW; *SOPHISTICATED* TELEMARKETING IS!

Telephone selling has been around for a long, long time, although phone companies would like us to think that they invented it and called it "telemarketing." The phone has been used for years to sell everything from newspaper and magazine subscriptions, to tickets for the policeman's ball, to special retail sales of all kinds. Almost invariably, companies that have exploited the phone have found it an extremely profitable avenue. In fact, it has been so successful that, until now, firms could afford to use just about any sort of telephone "pitch" or technique, and a certain number of prospects would buy if the appeal sounded at all reasonable.

The reason people would buy is because out of any population of prospects a certain number are probably actively or passively looking for what you have to offer, and they'll be glad you called. Even if your talk is terrible, some will nonetheless "take the sale away from you," and reward you with a purchase.

This is also known as the Law of Large Numbers, which says: Do enough of anything, and some of it has to be successful. Because we can speak with so many people over the phone within a short period of time, we are bound to get some sales.

There is trouble on the horizon, though. With the explosion of interest that has occurred in telephone selling, the phone wires are buzzing with appeals from all kinds of companies. Most telephone salespeople are real turn-offs for customers, as we'll point out in a different section of this book. This means that people are getting more calls and are becoming more resistant by having more opportunities to practice saying "no."

To be successful in the near future, we're going to have to

become much more sophisticated in penetrating customer resistance. This means that our appeals will have to be constructed upon unique principles that are customized to the population we're calling. Along with reading the *Wall Street Journal* and various trade publications, we'll want to look into such esoteric periodicals as the *Journal of Social Psychology* and conduct computer searches to determine where there is new knowledge appropriate to our sales mission.

Why bother with all of this? I'll give you an example. There may be no industry more resented than the aluminum siding industry, if you listen to the scores of talk shows that I do across North America, where average citizens call in to gripe about telephone selling. I can usually count on receiving at least one or two calls from irate people who claim that aluminum siding people are trying to sell them, and they own *brick* homes.

To my knowledge, the aluminum siding industry is not using very sophisticated telecommunications techniques. If they were aware of certain communications research, they would select a two-sided message strategy in building their talks. A two-sided message takes into account the resistance that people feel toward a product or firm, with the sales strategy reflecting this fact. This means that I would develop a strategy that would have a salesperson *acknowledge* people's resistance toward the message before proceeding to the heart of the sale.

Here is an example of a two-sided message:

Salesperson: Hello, Mr. Jones? This is Gary Goodman with Goodman Siding here in Glendale. How are you?
Jones: Not interested.
Salesperson: Well, I appreciate that, and you probably get a lot of calls like this. Am I right?
Jones: Sure do, and I usually end up hanging up on 'em!
Salesperson: I don't blame you, because you probably hear the same pitch over and over, right?

Where does the salesperson go from here? He or she can become dissociated from the typical telephone solicitor by simply continuing the sales appeal or by pointing out that *this* call is going to be different. As you can tell from the exchange between Jones and the salesperson, the negativity coming from the prospect has been greatly reduced, if not altogether diffused. How did this happen?

From the beginning of the call the prospect was made a "partner" in the sales process. His feelings were "valued" enough by the salesperson to be discussed openly. A sense of control was given to the prospect, which said, "I respect that you have power, Mr. Jones, and that I only have the privilege of speaking as long as you allow me to do so." The mood of the call was totally different than the typical, one-sided solicitation that is common in much of telephone selling, today.

A two-sided message strategy must be used in certain circumstances only, otherwise it can boomerang on us. If we use this appeal when there is no negativity fostered by the prospect, we can *introduce* problems where none existed before.

I recall purchasing a luxury car a few years ago when a salesperson really blew the deal by using a two-sided message when he shouldn't have. I was calling various dealers to get prices on a particular model, and I ended up with a salesman who thought he was pretty sharp. I said I was interested in a car that had been quoted to me as costing a certain amount of money. He said, "That's not possible." I said, "It sure is, and if you can't do better, I'm going to buy it." He said, "You don't mean the car at Alhambra Porsche-Audi, do you, because that already has two hundred miles on it! "

I said, "I sure do," and I rushed off the phone with him and called Alhambra Porsche-Audi, who gave me a great deal. You see, before this fellow had mentioned it, I didn't know Alhambra Porsche-Audi even existed!

Where did I learn about two-sided message strategies, and the circumstances under which they work and fail? From communications research that I did when studying for my Ph.D. in communications from the University of Southern California. I bring it up here to show you that there is "nothing as practical as a good theory," as a scientist Karl Popper once said, and this is especially the case when it comes to finding competitive advantages in the arena of telemarketing. Seat-of-the-pants wisdom, no matter how dearly paid for through years of experience in telephone selling, cannot approach the value of sophisticated, state-of-the-art knowledge in psychology, business, and communications, and for this reason we need to make our appeals stand out from the rest of the pack that is rushing into telemarketing.

DO YOU SPEAK "TELEPHONE"?

Telephone communication is unique. There are certain modes of expression that are appropriate for teleselling that have no place in face-to-face selling and vice versa. Walk into any successful phoneroom where numbers of salespeople are working and you'll hear styles of communication that are refreshing and novel.

You'll find that there is a great sense of intimacy and warmth created almost at the beginning of telephone calls. Some salespeople take the liberty to call presidents of companies by their first names, rather than waiting for a signal that this is okay. Some crack jokes and make people who are normally quite uptight feel at ease and have a good time.

Some salespeople use "phone-names," just as actors use stage names. They do this for various reasons. Their real names may be hard to pronounce or may not be as memorable as, say, "Bob Parker," or "Mary King," or "Sally Stewart." Many of those who use pseudonyms say that they feel a sense of role distance in what they are doing. This makes them bolder and less fearful of rejection. If people say "no" to Mary Stewart, they are rejecting a message and not someone's real identity.

In some phone rooms, you'll see salespeople standing on top of their desks while making their pitches. Ask them why they choose this perch and they'll tell you that they feel they are in command of the selling situation and feel "on top of things."

Some phone rooms use bells to signal when people have gotten sales, so when you hear a lot of chiming, it resembles the sound of old-fashioned cash registers at work. Pavlov would feel right at home amidst all of these reinforcements!

Many of the most successful salespeople use very casual language when selling because it sounds "like the way people talk." Though not completely grammatical, this sort of language gets the job done in making prospects feel that salespeople are sincere and spontaneous. For instance, salespeople may compose presentations that ask, "How ya doin'?" instead of the more formal, "How are you?" which can sound stilted and non-genuine.

Telephone language is also interesting because it is condensed. It packs a lot of wallop into very few words, because listeners tend to be impatient when using the phone. We have to say it fast, or run the risk of becoming involuntarily disconnected. A five-minute telephone sales pitch can sound like the equivalent of an hour-and-a-half personal presentation. Perhaps the ideal length of a telesales call is about three and a half minutes. This means that to be successful, our language needs to be snappy and graphic.

THE ROLLS-ROYCE OF TELEMARKETING

If it sounds like telemarketing operations must have a circus-like quality about them, this isn't so. Many of the most elegant products and services in the world are being sold by phone, with all of the decorum that one might expect from traffic in such trade.

Charles D. Schmitt is the St. Louis representative of Rolls-Royce Motors, and he has brought a unique style and flair to selling this most prestigious line of motorcars. In addition to using aggressive pricing practices, which rankle his fellow dealers, Schmitt breaks with automotive tradition by selling fully 20 percent of his vehicles by telephone. He keeps a beeper with him at all times, and he uses a 24-hour answering service to make sure he dosen't miss any serious customer inquiries. (the *Wall Street Journal*, May 24, 1983).

Schmitt seems to recognize that it doesn't matter if you are selling a $150,000 luxury car or a $15 book. If you are clever, motivated and informed, *you can sell anything by telephone.*

IF THE PHONE IS SO EFFECTIVE, WHY ISN'T EVERYONE USING IT TO GET RICH?

Most people are ignorant of the power of the telephone. Just as we have mentioned that there is a certain telephone language, there is also telephone illiteracy.

Most people have been insufficiently trained in the use of the phone for commercial purposes. Ask average people if they have ever had formal training with this tool, and you'll find that their "lessons," if they had any, stopped with the indoctrination received from Mom and Dad. When parents were telling us about this marvelous tool, they pointed out the need to "get off it as soon as possible," lest we run up a big bill. I believe we have come to equate telecommunication with punishment, because so many of us were chastised for spending too much time on the line, and for failing to do "important" things.

We have also come to think of talking on the phone as "a piece of cake" that any child can do effectively. This thinking overlooks the fact that there are very subtle phenomena occurring in telephone calls about which most people never have an inkling.

Take the beginning of a phone call, for instance. This is a crucial time at which the power relationship between participants in the conversation is forged. Many of us ignore the tone of voice that another person uses at the beginning of the call. That is, we ignore it on a conscious level. Unconsciously, we are tracking the tone very closely, and what we tend to do is match the tone we are hearing. While this can be very effective in a number of places in the call, it can get us into trouble if the tone of the voice we are hearing is depressed.

If someone sounds as if he or she is on a "bummer," we should pull the other person out of the blues by contrasting our voices with his or hers. This is accomplished by making our voice tone go up at the ends of certain words and lines, instead of down, where most depressing-sounding sentiments go. If addressing the person by name, don't flatly say, "Hello, Bill." This sounds conclusionary and gives the voice a downcast quality. Phrase the greeting as a question, instead. "Hello, Bill???" This will pick up your voice and his.

What happens next is one of the greatest little telecommunications events around. Bill will usually respond, "Yes!" His enthusiasm will be immediate and audible to you, and you'll find that instead of your call having to be an uphill battle to win his positive regard, you'll be able simply to sustain a pleasurable tone that was created in the first few seconds of the call.

Dale Carnegie used to say, "Act enthusiastic, and you'll be enthusiastic." Stanislavsky, the great acting teacher, used to coach his students in the fine art of preparing for the stage. He'd tell them essentially the same thing. Project your imaginary body onto the stage before your physical body gets there. Imagine the scene you are playing before you utter a word and see the whole event as being extraordinarily successful.

By inducing the prospect to sound enthusiastic, we cause the person to feel the same way. Social scientists explain this interesting shift in attitude as resulting from our need for cognitive consistency. If we sense ourselves acting in a certain manner, we tend to "explain to ourselves" that we must feel that way, too.

In a later section we'll look at how voice tone can be used in many different ways to control conversations unobtrusively and accomplish our goals. Tone tells us, though, that teleselling is a subtle craft that requires conscious refinement.

PINK ELEPHANTS
LOOK BETTER OVER THE PHONE

If you are looking for needles in haystacks, it always makes sense to bring a magnet along to help you. The same thing applies if we are trying to sell "oddball" goods or services. We need to use the best tool around, and there is no better one than the phone.

The phone helps to make immediate and significant contact with potential customers. It compels people to make decisions and make them fast. If you want to unload merchandise to just the right kind of person, the phone promises to be the most economical way of achieving your goal.

Carl was in the audiotape business for a few years and times turned tough for him. Customers were thinning out, and the ones who were buying, weren't paying on time. Add to this the fact that he was being assaulted by competition, and you have a perfect recipe for failure.

He had invested in very expensive tape-duplicating equipment for which he had to find a willing market. He struggled to come up with a potential buyer for his "pink elephants." After a number of unsuccessful personal visits to contacts in the recording industry, he decided in desperation to turn to the telephone. He figured that if he had to sell some pink elephants, he'd better parade them before as many potential customers as possible.

He found an industrial directory that listed the names, addresses, and phone numbers of likely prospects. Within ten hours of calling, he sold two duplicating machines at a price of $25,000 a piece. His troubles were over, and he learned a lesson about the power of the phone.

PRESIDENTIAL PERSUASION

In the 1960s, a fellow living in a small town in Texas was known for his boasting. He'd tell his friends around the crackerbarrel near the old post office how he was going to do this and that to make his fortune. His buddies, who really liked the guy, learned to discount his wild claims and promises and simply enjoy him for who he was, and not for who and what he promised to become.

If there was one subject that was this fellow's "religion," it was his beloved Dallas Cowboys, who could do no wrong, especially because they were going to be playing in the Super Bowl within about a week and a half. True to form, he started telling his friends that "I'm going to go to that Super Bowl, somehow!" This was equivalent to saying he was going to sprout wings and start airline service, because the game had been sold out, and scalpers were getting a ransom for tickets.

His friends felt that he had gone too far with this claim, and they tried gently to let him know that they wouldn't be disappointed if he couldn't make it to the game after all. In the meantime, the boaster was looking through the newspaper for a clue as to how he might get to the event. Suddenly, as he was reading a bland report about President Lyndon Johnson, he came up with his grand idea.

The president was scheduled for a round of tests at Bethesda Naval Hospital, which the article said would take about two weeks to complete. As Johnson's loyal constituent read this item, his mind did a few fast calculations.

"If he's going to be there for two weeks, there's no way that he can get to the Super Bowl, and presidents always have tickets, so why can't I have his?"

With so little time remaining until the game, he decided to pick up the phone and call the hospital. Speaking to one of the president's aides, the fellow explained his idea and asked that a ticket be mailed to him, if possible.

Within a few days, a crisp Super Bowl ticket arrived in the mail, and our friend was as elated as his friends were stunned. He demonstrated that you can not only reach out and sell someone, but sell the *one* person who has the power to reward you with what you are looking for, even if the person is a president of the United States!

IS THE TRAVELING SALESMAN COMING TO THE END OF THE ROAD?

According to recent data, the average cost of an industrial sales call is between $160 and $300, whether a sale is made or not. This means that more and more companies can no longer afford the luxury of sending out their minions to press the flesh with potential customers.

Monsanto, among countless other companies, is experimenting with the substitution of telephone salespeople for field salespeople. Representatives in its plastic bottles division are assigned to marginal accounts or to customers who are in remote locations. The company has found that it is still able to convey a personal touch through its telemarketers by setting up regular times each month for telephone appointments. Through this device, they have a chance of delivering a *higher* standard of service to customers than before, by virtue of increased contacts.

This company has overcome customer resistance to the change in method by introducing the program through a series of letters touting the benefits of telemarketing, which include greater savings for the buyer. Moreover, Monsanto printed the picture of each representative on all pieces of correspondence mailed to customers, which gives the feeling that one is working with someone who is flesh and blood, and not simply a disembodied voice.

2001: A PHONE ODYSSEY

One of the newest devices in telemarketing seems like something straight out of the movie *2001: A Space Odyssey*. It is a computer that automatically dials certain programmed sequences of phone numbers and proceeds to make pitches to "live" humans.

One of these robots has been named "Hal," and what it has been designed to do is ask a series of questions, after having greeted the person on the other end. It pauses long enough for the responses to go "on tape," which are examined at the end of the day by the sponsoring company. This way, the robot does the prospecting while humans need only listen to the beautiful music of people who responded favorably and want further information.

While some folks are shocked to receive a computer-generated call, it seems that most are at least a little intrigued. You'd be amazed at the number of people who carry on very pleasant "conversations" with the computer, as if it were human.

From a selling standpoint, the computer seems to be a plus. It never grows tired or impatient. Its presentations are uniform and unchanging, thus lending the sales message to scientific analysis and measurement. And the computer never takes a coffee break, or calls in sick. At least, not yet. . . .

With the coming of age of computers in the field of telemarketing, we may find that not only can *you* sell anything by telephone, but a machine may be able to, also!

SEEING ISN'T NECESSARILY BELIEVING

Imagine calling someone on the phone, and in a period of less than three minutes, asking the person to buy a piece of fine art, valued at $2000, that the person hasn't seen before, by an artist with whom the prospect may be unfamiliar.

Difficult? Definitely. Impossible? Not on your life. It has been done, and it is being done by a number of art galleries in California and elsewhere.

What's the secret? All products and services can be sold by telephone if we merely become informed about the various methods that have been proven to get results. This book will explain these procedures to you and point out that you have within your fingertips a way of coming up with just the right appeal, with just the right "tone," for the right audience.

But let's get back to art. Art *seems* like a difficult sale because it involves seeing a work, aesthetic or artistic appreciation on the part of a buyer, and a judgment as to whether the piece under consideration would fit into someone's office or living room. The sale involves quite a few dollars, as well.

These are some of the obstacles that could get in our way. Perhaps the biggest one hasn't been articulated yet in this chapter. This is the idea that certain things can be and others cannot be sold by phone. I've heard this claim over the years from countless salespeople who believe that there is some sort of chemical reaction that occurs in a face-to-face presentation that "simply can't happen on the phone."

If they believe this to be true, it *will be true for them.* This is what is referred to as a self-fulfilling prophesy, or a self-sealing proposition. I have seen extraordinary things sold by phone, and I've helped a number of companies design winning procedures for accomplishing their ambitions. In all cases, *someone thought it could be done.*

As you'll see later, art isn't terribly difficult to sell if we use the winning formula that I'll set forth for you. You'll see that a piece of art is only as "abstract" and "intangible" as your talents will make it appear to a buyer. You'll also discover that it may be an advantage *not* to have the piece in front of the prospect, because his or her initial reaction may be uninformed by the "deeper value" that you'll be able to discuss over the phone. In other words, seeing isn't *necessarily* believing.

A TELEPHONE, A TRACTOR, AND THE RUSSIAN REVOLUTION

Several years ago when I was in the book business a fellow worked for me, selling various libraries by phone. He was very creative, but more important, he was extremely observant and enthusiastic. As you'll see, he had a sense of humor, too.

He was so good at using our pitch that he decided to alter it in some absurd ways. We were selling books on the history of the West and on various nature topics. He figured that our pitch was so good that he could sell anything with it, and he set out to prove his point.

He walked up to me one day and said, "Boss, I've invented a new library that's bound to be a bestseller. Want to hear some titles?"

My interest was piqued and I said, "Sure."

"Well," he continued, "It's called the Industrial Library, and the lead book that we'll be selling will be called *Soot*."

"Soot?" I couldn't believe what I was hearing.

"That's right; *Soot*."

"Why *Soot*?"

"*Soot* is a terrific title because it's suggestive of industry, in its gritty, grimy reality. Don't judge the title, though," he insisted.

"What do you suggest I do?" I asked.

"Let me sell a few for you, and you'll see what I mean!"

Well, I couldn't resist. He pulled from his shirt pocket a

hand-scrawled presentation that took off from the one we were already using. All he did was plug in descriptions of his new titles, and he let the form of the patterned talk do the rest of the work for him.

He got a person on the phone, and the next thing I knew, he was pitching her as if he had said the same words a million times before. He said: "Mrs. Jones, we have an exciting new series called the Industrial Library, and our lead book is called, *Soot. Soot* takes you back to the industrial revolution when the might of the modern world was forged. Back to the days of Dickens' England and little David Copperfield. Back to the coal mines and the robber barons of big oil. You'll be taken step by step through the events that took America from the prairie into the factory, from innocence to urban sophistication.

"And, Mrs. Jones, you'll be able to look forward to other great books in the Industrial Library, such as *The Silo,* and one of my favories, *The Tractor.* You'll learn how tractors helped to win the Russian Revolution. . . . "

And he went on, from one glorious claim to the next, until he asked for the sale and got it! We were absolutely amazed that a tongue-in-cheek presentation could be as effective as he made it. I recall that he made about ten "test calls" and he ended up selling at least half of them.

My associate proved that you can even sell "absurd" products, if you follow a winning format, and if you cultivate performative abilities. He also demonstrated that the phone is an ideal way to test market an idea without having to gear up and produce an end product, unless the market requires it.

WINE TASTING BY PHONE

There is a maxim in selling that says you will be successful to the extent that you engage the customer's *senses*. If he or she can touch, see, smell, hear, or taste what you are offering, your products will lend themselves naturally to being experienced in a sensual manner.

By this same reasoning, numbers of people have been discouraged from selling sensual products by phone because they have thought that the absence of fragrance, feel, and appearance put them at a disadvantage. This isn't necessarily so, as you'll see.

There is a firm in California that sells fine wines by telephone. In one sense, people "get a taste" of the product through clever descriptions that are conveyed by the telemarketers. People are told that the wines have a wonderful bouquet. They hear about all of the wonderful entrees that are complemented by certain selections. And they are told they should "reserve a few cases now, while they are still available."

Every now and then the company sponsors in-home winetasting parties that the telemarketers set up, and which are highly successful. What enables them to market wine without the wine-tasting privilege?

This company understands the enchanting nature of the auditory channel of communication. In the same ways that radio programs used to captivate the imaginations of people listening to the Lone Ranger and Buck Rogers, we can create marvelous effects by artistically designing our appeals so that people feel a similar sense of immediacy and interest.

NOW YOU HEAR IT; NOW YOU DON'T: THE ROLE OF *MAGIC* IN TELEPHONE SELLING

If we ask salespeople to name those fields to which selling is akin, they'll usually mention psychology, athletics, teaching, and, perhaps, religion, among other things. Few will mention magic, though this "dark art" is very much related to selling, generally, and telephone selling, specifically.

Telephone salespeople don't have to pull bunnies out of hats to benefit from the illusionist's art. Effective phone people orchestrate a series of actions that create an illusion for an audience through such techniques as redirection and distraction. By doing so, they reduce resistance and create an atmosphere of acceptance.

Our voices can produce very subtle magical effects. There are two basic aspects of voice: content and tone. Research indicates that when these elements are in contradiction, as they are when someone is sarcastic, we believe the voice more than we do the content in arriving at an interpretation of the overall message. For instance, if I said, "I really like you," and my voice wasn't perceived as sincere, it wouldn't matter that the content was conveying a positive message. The idea that would come through to the listener would be that I doubted the accuracy of that which my content was declaring.

This phenomenon can be used beneficially by salespeople. When mentioning the price of our products and services, we are at the weakest point in our presentations. Our voices reflect vulnerability by growing heavy and burdened, or by giving off a sense of insecurity or reluctance on our part to discuss costs. Clients pick up on our feelings, and while we may be saying that the price of the product is "very reasonable at two hundred dollars," our tone may be disputing this.

What we should do is *create an illusion* of reasonableness by making our voices sound light instead of heavy. Our tone should be saying, "This is really a pittance, Mr. Smith, and I wouldn't give the price a second thought, if I were you." This technique will *distract* the customer from the cost by focusing attention upon our voices.

By structuring our sales appeal in various ways, we can redirect the attention of the customer. For instance, the after-mailing approach, which we'll discuss in detail in a later chapter, asks the person if he or she recalls receiving a letter or brochure from us in the mail. While searching through the memories of mailers-past, the person is forgetting about resisting our influence, and is becoming *actively involved* in the success of our call, although he or she is unaware of how this is occurring at the moment.

There are several other techniques for controlling sales calls in subtle ways, which will propel you toward your overall objective of closing the order while encountering as little resistance as possible.

A SHOCKING EXPERIMENT

A behavioral scientist performed an experiment some time ago that tells us a lot about the futility of conventional face-to-face selling, in some cases, and the relative effectiveness and simplicity of using the phone to make customer contacts.

He built a cage that was about two feet long and two feet high. At the front of the cage was an opening, into which he could place his experimental subjects, which were rats. In the middle of the cage, at the bottom, was an electric plate that conducted a mild amount of current when the scientist threw a switch. At the back of the cage was a food dispenser, which was stocked with tasty cheese treats.

The experimenter began his round of activities by taking the rat and placing it inside the cage. What the rat did next was predictable. It saw and smelled the cheese and immediately ran toward it. As it got to the center of the cage, the experimenter threw the electric switch, and the rat responded to the jolt by flipping backwards in the air, and then by continuing toward its goal, the cheese. When it arrived at the food dispenser, it was rewarded with a cheese morsel.

The experimenter repeated the exact procedure. The rat was placed in the cage; it started toward the food; it received a shock; it flipped backwards in the air; and it received a reward in the form of cheese.

The third time around, though, the experimenter changed things slightly. He placed the rat in the cage, as before, but instead of activating the electroplate, the experimenter allowed the rat to touch the surface without being shocked. Guess what happened next? *The rat flipped in the air, anyway!* The rat "learned," through the first experiences, that the flipping behavior caused the reward to come. It thought there was a cause-and-effect relationship between flipping and eating, when in reality, this had nothing to do with the dispensing of the food. The *experimenter* caused the food to be given. This was something that the rat didn't account for in its analysis of the situation. The rat simply thought that in repeating every behavior that preceded the reward it would cause another reward to come.

This is exactly what traditional salespeople do when they insist on engaging in elaborate behavioral sequences before asking a customer for an agreement. Some salespeople convince themselves that they have to wine and dine all prospects before getting down to business. They may be performing a series of ten behaviors when only one or two are really causing most of their success to accrue.

The *Wall Street Journal* recently ran an article on a successful stock brokerage company that services small towns as its specialty. An interview with a top salesman determined that he makes a point of visiting people in person at their farms or homes while discussing "everything but" an order. He follows up with them by mail through the device of a short and friendly note that says he's happy to have spoken with them. Several weeks later, *he calls them by phone and asks them for an order.* If we asked him what it is in his ritual that *really* sells folks, what do you think he would say? He'd point to the personal visit and the letter and discount the significance of the phone, *although that was the medium he chose for the purpose of closing the deal!*

Who knows how many more deals he would close if he would reduce his personal visits and letter-writing and concentrate on telephone contact? Unless someone instructs him otherwise, he'll go on "wasting time," while thinking this is what is causing his sales to occur.

A HAIR-RAISING (AND MONEY-RAISING) STORY

Quite by accident, one of the most successful businessmen in the wig business in America gave himself a lesson on the power of the telephone. He had taken a plane to see some prospects in a distant town when he found that he was getting rejected by one after the other. Feeling depressed, he started toward the airport before finishing his round of visits. He felt so defeated that he was going to forget about seeing the last prospect on his list.

Ten minutes before his plane was to take him home, he decided it would only be polite to tell the prospect not to expect him. Suddenly, an idea came to him. Instead of making his departure a "minus," why couldn't he turn it into a plus? This is exactly what he did.

He called his prospect and said that his schedule was so busy that he wasn't going to be able to see him after all, and if the customer wished to place an order, he'd have to do it right on the spot, on the phone. To the salesman's surprise, he closed a several-thousand-dollar deal that moment, and upon his return he immediately installed a telephone sales unit in his firm. Now, the business he generates by phone extends into the millions of dollars each year! And to think that he came within a hair of simply getting on that plane .

THE PHONE IS FASTER THAN THE FOOT

Have you ever noticed what happens when you are sitting in an executive's office and the telephone rings? It gets answered, doesn't it? More times than otherwise, no matter what the nature of the face-to-face meeting happens to be, the phone will receive priority and be answered, at the expense of whatever is being discussed by the folks in the room.

This is disconcerting to some people, of course, but it is an advantage to the telemarketer. When there is a contest between someone who is in our presence who wants to speak to us and someone on the phone, the phone person usually receives priority because that form of communication is fleeting, and no one wants to miss what could be an excellent opportunity.

THE TWENTY-SECOND SALES PRESENTATION

When I decided to go into consulting on a full-time basis, after having taught college for five years at the University of Southern California, California State University, Northridge, and DePauw University, I reached out to sell a number of organizations by phone as my way of getting my business going.

I contacted several colleges, companies, and other organizations, and within a twenty-second presentation I enlisted their help in sponsoring my telephone effectiveness and telemarketing training seminars. I asked them to invest, in many cases, thousands of dollars on a caller who was unknown to them.

I was extremely successful. So successful, in fact, that my programs came to be offered by thirty-five universities and several Fortune-500 companies as well as by trade associations from coast to coast. I accomplished in a period of several months what would have taken a lifetime to do if I had tried to use face-to-face persuasion.

You'll have a chance to evaluate my "twenty-second special" in a later chapter, and I'm sure you'll find it as powerful as I did when you put it into practice.

WE'RE ALL TELEPHONE SALESPEOPLE

If you are a butcher, baker, or candlestick maker, you are also a telephone salesperson if you have any customer contact through this medium. Simply by speaking to potential customers, you are encouraging them or discouraging them from doing business with your firm.

As we all know, secretaries are particularly powerful in their influence over the phone. They often inadvertently "give away" the true feelings of their firm toward us through their tone of voice. If *they* sound unhappy to hear from us, especially if we have been doing business with their company for some time, we can be assured that their principals feel likewise, though they are more careful to conceal their true sentiments.

In my most recent book, *Selling Skills for the Non Salesperson*, I discussed the importance of selling ourselves as well as enhancing the image of our organizations, even if we feel we aren't formal "salespeople." It's up to us to use our considerable powers of persuasion to influence customers and prospects through each contact.

In the next chapter, you'll learn how to sell yourself by telephone. You will learn how to exploit the subtleties of the phone that can help you to get the most out of every opportunity.

As we move through this book, remember one thing: You can sell *anything* by telephone!

CHAPTER TWO

HOW TO SELL YOURSELF OVER THE PHONE

When you think about it, the odds would seem to be stacked against telephone salespeople.

As far as 'most prospects are concerned, they are only disembodied voices coursing through telephone wires, but they still sell.

Moreover, as company after company dives into telemarketing it becomes increasingly difficult to distinguish yourself from the rest of the folks who are trying to make a living by using this rediscovered business tool.

Perhaps the most urgent challenge facing telemarketers is that of appearing credible before those with whom we are speaking. The old adage that to sell something, "you have to first sell yourself," definitely applies to telephone selling.

How can we market our personalities when we have only a few seconds in order to establish rapport? How can we persuade otherwise busy people to listen patiently to our story and various claims about products and services, when it is so easy to hang up instead and cast us into electronic oblivion? How can we avoid sounding like carnival barkers, as so many unprofessional telephone salespeople do?

My company does a lot of consulting work for various industries. I have noticed one flaw in the delivery of most inexperienced or ineffective salespeople: They rush through their talk.

This is especially so at the beginning of the presentation, when they are announcing themselves and their companies.

"HellothisisGaryGoodmanwithGoodmanCommunications howareyou," sounds like a blur, instead of a proud announcement of one's name and affiliation. If there is any time during which we should sound composed, it is at the very start of the conversation.

This is the time when people ask themselves the fateful question: "Am I going to like this call or am I going to dislike it?"

When we hear someone who is rushing, the person seems out of control. Professionals, if they have no other significant quality, seem to be in charge at all times. They don't get ruffled or easily distracted. They focus upon a target, and all of their energies are directed at the bull's-eye. If they miss, as everyone does, they collect themselves and try again.

REAL PROFESSIONALS
LIKE THEMSELVES, AND IT SHOWS

My training seminars usually begin with short self-introductions. Participants mention their names, background, and a brief statement of their goal in the session. I am always fascinated with the various ways that people articulate their own names.

The emphasis one gives to one's own name can tell the listener a lot about the person. Does the person think well of him or herself? Not if the name sounds garbled or too soft to be easily heard. Is the name rushed through? This could mean that the person doesn't have very high self-esteem.

If the person is comfortable with the name, it will sound very smooth and pleasing to the ear. This is a pretty good index as to how the person views him or herself, and it is good to remember that it takes a pretty strong ego to surpass the obstacles presented in the telemarketing situation.

HOW TO BECOME AN
ATTRACTIVE PHONE PERSONALITY

I enjoy doing radio and television talk shows and I feel a special kinship with their hosts. Most of these folks have had extensive voice training, which enables them to make even the most dreary subject sparkle.

You might be surprised at the number of radio hosts who have formerly been telephone salespeople while they were in college or at some other period in their development. These folks are really "naturals" because their voices are their fortunes, and they know how to make the most out of them.

One thing I have noticed is the way radio people greet me when I am being introduced on the air. Without fail, it is with what I might term "polished enthusiasm" and a sense of "positive expectancy" about the outcome of the interview. This is contagious. I feel immediately that they are trying their hardest while investing confidence in my abilities to communicate. We create a performative bond, seemingly within moments, that says, "Let's make this program a real success."

A successful telephone sales presentation proceeds as well on a foundation of cooperation between client and salesperson. This is something that most folks don't appreciate because they are too busy upholding the fiction that the sales process is a "battle," where entrenched forces are rallied against each other, and one party emerges a winner and the other the loser.

Cooperation is one of the major keys to selling on a professional level. The time to engineer this sort of mutuality is at the beginning of the call. In the same way that media personalities make us feel comfortable by saying our names with "polished enthusiasm" and a "positive expectancy," we should utter the names of prospects in the same manner.

When a prospect comes on the line, we should say the person's name as if we were asking a question, as we would when saying, "Hello, Bill?" This will give our voice a lift and it will sound to Bill as if we are really interested in speaking to him, and not to any old person who might give us an order.

Normally, we tend to greet a person who comes on the line with a flat "reading" of his or her name with an atonal quality, as in, "Oh, hello, Bill." This can make it sound as if we are a little disappointed in speaking to him.

USE A LITTLE SOCIAL PSYCHOLOGY

There has been a lot of research in the area of "interpersonal attraction theory," which explores why people like or dislike each other. For folks who crave simplicity, this area of inquiry is especially satisfying because it offers some basic insights that we can apply to the selling process.

How can we make someone like us? "Like them first," researchers tell us. It's just that simple.

If we can demonstrate that we like the party with whom we are speaking on the phone, the odds are very good that the person will "like us back," and we'll be rewarded with sales.

SEND THEM A TELEPHONE SMILE

By smiling when we are talking on the phone, we can send to prospects the message "we like you." It is really simple to do, and you will be amazed at how much more smoothly our calls seem to progress. There is evidence that people can tell with 90 percent accuracy whether we have positive or negative attitudes toward them, simply by listening to our voices!

BE LIKE YOUR PROSPECTS

My dad spent many years in the advertising business, and he would often talk about the sometimes strange rituals that people in that profession would go through in order to get and keep accounts. If an advertising agency had Chevrolet as a major account, what kind of car do you think agency representatives were expected to drive? Fords?

Only if they wanted to be on the streets driving to their next place of employment! All senior-level people were expected to drive cars manufactured by their clients. This could get a little absurd as the agency would lose a Chevy account and pick up a Ford account. Expensive as it was, senior staffers were pressured into selling their old standbys for new models.

Clearly, ad agencies wish to create a sense of *identification* with their clients, and this makes a lot of sense because *we tend to buy from people who are like us in significant ways*.

For years IBM and a number of Fortune-500 companies insisted that executives and salespeople wear crisp white shirts and ties. This apparel was to tell prospects, "we are professional." There was tremendous ego involvement in the uniform, and "outsiders" who didn't conform to this model were frowned upon. In fact, if you wanted to sell some of these companies something, you needed to adopt the same dress style to encourage them to feel that they were like you, and that you were "safe" to do business with.

Some of these rules have been relaxed a bit over the years, but smart salespeople still tend to look a little more formal than they have to when dealing with large firms. If you ask them if it helps sales, they'll tell you, "You bet!"

Although we can't really influence folks over the phone based upon our clothing choices, we still have to be good at the task of creating identification with them. The fact that we can't use *visual symbols* to help our cause merely makes the process more subtle and more challenging.

BECOME A *DYNAMIC* LISTENER

Most of us think of listening as a very boring activity. We'd rather talk than listen, and this may be especially true of salespeople, who are cursed with the gift of gab.

Great salespeople learn to be great listeners. They teach

themselves to listen for what is and isn't being said, so that they can adjust their sales message for maximal effect.

Telephonic listening is supremely important because people are giving us cues that can put lots of dollars in our pockets if we tune into them properly.

What are some of the subtle nuances that we should be listening for? Start with the *regional influences* that are in the voice.

I was speaking to a stockbroker the other day who had a distinctive Bostonian speech pattern in his delivery. He pronounced the word "half" as if it were "hoff." This was one tipoff that he was from New England. He also pronounced his "r's" as if they were "ah's."

I was able to get a "fix" on his dialect within a few sentences, and this helped me to develop a strategy for relating to the fellow. I chose a certain pattern of humor that I felt was "Eastcoastish," and we got along famously. He probably ended up feeling more comfortable with the conversation than he would have otherwise.

By sensing his native region I was able to tap into a zone of psychological comfort for him and relate to him on a deeper level than I would have if I hadn't been listening for this information. Sometimes, it helps us if we stop in the middle of a chat and ask, "Are you originally from Boston?" Usually, people are impressed that we were listening closely enough to hazard such a guess, and they can then feel free to talk about their "old turf " which they might miss.

I recall asking a woman if she was from Wisconsin; she nearly fell off her chair because she had lived in California for about twenty years and she said, "I thought I lost any accent I had."

There are other cues for which we should be on the alert, including the overall intensity with which people speak. If you are speaking to a "whisperer," don't blow the person away by using a big and booming delivery yourself. Adjust your volume to meet that to which you are listening.

Think about speaking on the phone as a musical act where your goal is to *harmonize* with the other person. To create beautiful music together, you don't want to drown a delicate violin with a thundering tuba, do you? Of course not.

At the same time, you should be concerned about your overall tonal pattern as it relates to *pitch*. Some people sound as if they are bored with the world. Their voices are flat and lifeless, and they seem to drone on from one sentence into the next. Although our "natural" voices may seem to be completely opposite of this style, it can make sense for us temporarily to adopt it in order to increase the comfort level of the prospect.

I was speaking before the national sales meeting of a large company when I was introduced to the head of corporate operations for the firm. I could tell that this fellow was more comfortable with numbers and graphs and charts than with social interaction, so I "cooled it a little" when it was time to get together for a talk.

My voice became rather restrained and low key, and if someone had taped our conversation, we might have sounded like brothers! We got along very well, and I sensed that he felt I was okay and that he could feel comfortable in sending more business my way.

I knew that the guy was a good fellow because I could read his nonverbal cues, or body language, and they told me that he was friendly enough, even if his voice lagged behind. Over the phone, many of us would have thought that this person was a "cold fish" who disliked us for some reason, and we might have become defensive as a result, which would have blown the deal.

This is why it is important to understand that people have different communication styles, and there is nothing wrong with this. Our task as effective telephone salespeople is to identify these styles through dynamic listening and then make our approaches complementary with those that we are hearing.

SELL YOURSELF
BY BEING "SOLD" YOURSELF

How can we convince others of the merit of something when we aren't "sold" ourselves? It's very difficult.

When we seem convinced that we have the best product or service on the planet, our enthusiasm lights up the people with whom we're speaking. I once heard a sales consultant claim that the single most powerful appeal that one could use when selling was more of an "attitude" than any particular statement.

The winning attitude that we need to give off is *confidence*. We can only be successful in getting others to show confidence in us if we already seem to feel that we are sure that what we are selling will do people a lot of good. Show the slightest doubt, and people will back out of deals right and left. How can we develop self-confidence?

One of the best ways to develop self-confidence is to tell yourself on a daily basis that you are doing wonderful things for people. I know this may seem overly self-congratulatory, but it is one of the most important methods of assuring your own success.

I deal with thousands of salespeople each year and I've come to recognize patterns to success as well as failure. Salespeople seem to fail because they lose that burning sense of certainty that prospects find irresistible.

Here are some of the statements that we should repeat to ourselves on a daily basis:

1. I have a wonderful product/service.
2. Countless people have benefited from my product/service.
3. My clients are going to be happy to hear from me.
4. By selling, I make the world a better place while improving the lives of countless people.
5. There is no other human being quite like me.
6. Selling is a means of promoting my personal and professional growth.
7. Nothing takes place in our economy until one person sells another person an idea, a product, or a service.
8. My clients expect me to be a leader and point out to them courses of action that I believe are going to result in benefits for both of us.
9. When clients express reservations or objections they are reacting out of fear and ignorance, and the best way of dealing with them is with patience and understanding.
10. If selling were easy, everyone would be doing it. The fact that selling is challenging is one of the reasons I enjoy it and am drawn to it.

Let's look at these statements in a little more detail.

1. *I have a wonderful product/service.* Surprising as it may sound, I know many veteran salespeople who are "burned out" in their jobs. They seem bored by the same old day-after-day routine, and if they weren't so financially committed to a given lifestyle, they would probably run off to the circus.

Much of their dissatisfaction stems from losing confidence in the quality of their products and services. We're all familiar with the idea that the shoemaker's children are the last to have their shoes repaired. In a similar way, salespeople are sometimes less "taken" with the merits of their own wares than the average customer, who sees them only for the first time. The salesperson becomes numbed to the glitter and allure of his or her stock to such an extent that it interferes in the fair representation of these items to other people.

This is why it is important for all of us to praise our products and services to ourselves before we ever pick up the phone to speak with a client. It's somewhat akin to learning the secret behind a magic trick. Before we know what the trick is we are as enchanted as the next person. Once the secret is shared with us we wonder why we never saw the manipulation before, and each additional time we see the trick, all we can focus upon is the "manipulation" involved.

We should let the magic "do its stuff" for these newcomers, who are also our customers. Don't stand in the way of someone who wants to buy something!

2. *Countless people have benefited from my product/ service.* There is an old expression that I learned many years ago of which I am particularly fond: "You never know where your influence stops." This seems particularly appropriate to the arena of selling.

Since my second book was published, (*Reach Out & Sell Someone*) I have received hundreds of letters, phone calls, and compliments about the book and the ideas on telephone selling that it contains. Most of the letters mention that readers are finding that they are making money with the ideas I presented, and they are finding their jobs a lot easier to perform after using the book.

This is all very gratifying, and sometimes I find myself lingering over a particular letter, while imagining how someone's life may have been affected by what I wrote. What I find really mind-boggling is the idea that someone's family and associates, and maybe thousands of people, might have been directly affected by my ideas.

Of course, I am a salesperson, and my books are, in some measure, attempts to sell my ideas. I need to remind myself that I may be doing a lot of good for a lot of people I'll never meet, but who will benefit directly from my products and services.

Whenever you feel a little low, remind yourself of the same thing. Countless people *are* benefiting from the products and services you are selling, and if they could thank you directly, they would.

3. *My clients are going to be happy to hear from me.* One of the major problems telephone salespeople need to get over is "call reluctance" or, as I have termed it in my book, *Winning by Telephone*, "phone fear."

I find that salespeople who are afraid of using the phone are victims of their own runaway imaginations. They imagine that the person on the other end of the line is either snarling at them or is secretly laughing at them. Fear of rejection and fear of embarrassment prevent countless salespeople from realizing their teleselling potential, and this needn't be the case.

A proven way of conquering phone fear is to imagine that the person with whom you are going to be speaking will be happy to hear from you. This will give your voice an upbeat sound, and *you'll probably create the outcome you have imagined.*

Think about the person who walks around all the time with a sign that reads, "Don't kick me." What do you think people are apt to do, respect the wishes expressed on the sign? Not really. They're probably more likely to kick the person because they want to see what happens, and because the sign-wearer was secretly asking for this to happen, anyway.

When we project the feeling that folks are not going to like the fact that we called, we end up inviting them to kick us "telephonically." Once again, sound positive and act as if people will be glad you called, and you'll be surprised at how often this comes true for you.

4. *By selling, I make the world a better place while improving the lives of countless people.* Selling may be one of the most poorly regarded callings around. Ask youngsters what they aspire to be, and I assure you that no one will say "salesperson," unless he or she has a parent in the field.

Simply put, selling gets a very bad rap in most places, which it doesn't deserve. Salespeople are many things to potential buyers, including educators. I recall having about a half hour to kill the other night when I was in the downtown area of Los Angeles. I decided to drop into the Bullocks-Wilshire department store.

This place is something else. Its Art Deco architecture is great to look at and it carries some very fine merchandise. I walked into a room that was completely dedicated to Steuben glass, some of the most interesting crystal in the world.

Not knowing anything about crystal at the time, I approached a salesperson and asked, "What would you say is the finest crystal in the world?" Her reaction was fantastic—I didn't have to say another word. She gave me a tour of the entire gallery of glass and explained why one brand was superior to the next, and by the time our thirty minutes together had elapsed, I left the store knowing a lot about glass and actually having some interest in becoming a collector.

Although it may take some time for me to turn my new knowledge into a hobby, I have already put what I have learned to use. There is no question that my life, in terms of my understanding of various art forms, has been improved by a salesperson, and if we think about it, this happens to all of us all the time.

5. *There is no other human being quite like me.* I know this sounds trite, but in an age of rampaging automation, when none of us knows whether he or she will be replaced by a machine, it is soothing to remind ourselves of this humble fact.

When times get tough for us we sometimes have only our character to fall back on in order to help us to "hang in there" until things improve. Remember that nothing is as valuable as your own personal resources: your energy, your intelligence, and your past record of accomplishments.

You constitute a unique accomplishment that transcends

your performance on any given day, before any given prospect. Remember this fact and you'll always feel "sold on yourself."

6. *Selling is a means of promoting my personal and professional growth.* You almost have to feel sorry for people who haven't sold a product or service to a customer. They have missed one of life's more exhilarating endeavors. How can you ever become bored when you are constantly matching wits with people, while struggling at the same time to outdo your preceding day's production?

Selling demands that we keep up with world events as well as with trends in various industries so that we can speak intelligently on a number of subjects and relate to our customers. You have to keep growing to continue to be an effective salesperson.

One of the pleasant rewards of selling comes from being able to accurately measure our performance over time. If we want to grow in respect to our production targets, our effectiveness can be charted with accuracy.

7. *Nothing takes place in our economy until one person sells another person an idea, a product, or a service.* Selling is the engine that drives our economy. I have a friend who developed a Theory of Surplus. His idea is that the economy grows only if people buy *more* than what they need at any given time. This generates jobs, which generate more consumption, and around and around the economy goes, with everyone ultimately prospering more than he or she would have if only necessities were purchased in modest amounts.

For people to buy in surplus amounts, there have to be salespeople who will accomodate their wishes. A number of marketing people have said that the fundamental purpose of a commercial enterprise is "the creation of a customer." There is no other person as central to this mission in our economy as the salesperson.

8. *My clients expect me to be a leader and point out to them courses of action that I believe are going to result in benefits for both of us.* The effective salesperson is someone who knows that his or her purpose is to persuade someone to do something that the person wouldn't have otherwise done. This means that salespeople tell other people what is good for them, and tell them with a good deal of conviction.

Some people don't want the responsibility of making decisions for other people, so they fail as salespeople. They feel that they would "rather let the prospect decide for himself" than run the risk of appearing at all "pushy." This really doesn't serve the cause of endearing the weak seller to the customer. It more frequently backfires, leaving the customer without a consultant upon whom to rely and disturbed over the prospect of having to risk making a decision for him or herself.

As already suggested, we have to appear *certain* to the prospect in order to gracefully transform the person into a customer. It is better to err on the side of making too many sales than too few, even if we seem to feel that there is some "nobility" involved in letting people talk themselves out of buying.

9. *When clients express reservations or objections they are reacting out of fear and ignorance, and the best way of dealing with them is with patience and understanding.* It is fair to say that salespeople fear objections and rejection more than just about anything else. Interruptions are avoided by fast-talking, which simply causes more frequent interruptions and rejection.

The best way to handle rejection, as we will discuss in detail in Chapter Four, is to treat it as if it were helpful to the sales process, and not a hindrance. For instance, if a person says, "I really don't need it," we shouldn't rush to justify why the item is necessary but instead *agree* with the prospect as a prelude to overcoming the resistance.

Most people are poorly informed about our products and services, yet they try to conceal this from us by putting up defenses and smoke screens. We'll lose business if we insist on fighting with them, when we can profitably involve them in selling themselves, as will be discussed later.

10. *If selling were easy, everyone would be doing it.* The fact that selling is challenging is one of the reasons I enjoy it and am drawn to it. I remember complaining to my boss during one of my first selling assignments. I said, "Jim, the people are pretty tough out there!"

He looked at me and replied, "Of course they are. If they weren't, why would we need you?"

He was right. Salespeople perform services that are necessary because most things don't sell themselves. They need someone actively touting them, while overcoming the natural reaction of people to say "no" to a new idea.

When I feel things are getting tough, I remind myself that I have chosen my career in large measure because it is challenging and because it takes rare skills and dedication to do effectively.

TOOTING YOUR OWN HORN, EVER SO SWEETLY

Many of us are uncomfortable when we talk about ourselves. This is especially the case when it comes to popping off about our accomplishments.

We have been given modesty lessons from the time we were tots so that we wouldn't seem brash or overly aggressive to other people. What this has done is make most of us "underrecognized" for our achievements and contributions.

Unless our prospects come to learn of our credibility, how are they to be influenced by it? One of the keys to selling ourselves is to appear dynamic to our clients. To do this, we need to let them know of our many successes so they'll have confidence in us.

Of course, we can't walk into a room or pick up the phone and simply announce, "I'm terrific," although we might think so. We have to be a little more subtle than that, while making sure that the message still comes across, loud and clear.

Here's how to get away with boasting: Don't do it! That's right. Have someone else do it while borrowing your voice.

Actually, it's simple. It's known as using a third-party testimonial. I could get into some trouble by saying, "My company did a great job with Xerox this year." This kind of statement would be blatantly self-serving and would bring too much attention to itself. Instead, I prefer to let Xerox "do the talking" by saying, "Our friends at Xerox were kind enough to say that they got a great deal out of our program and are looking forward to terrific long-term benefits from it."

This almost seems like a tribute to the firm for whom we did business, while the point isn't missed that Goodman Communications Corporation is known for doing excellent telephone training work. Similarly, we can build our credibility by being less specific in our statements. We can say, "We have been told by a number of clients that they wouldn't consider doing business with any other firm." This appeal has the power of saying, "Get on the bandwagon: What's good for them is good for you, too."

BE BRIEF, BE BRILLIANT, AND BE *DONE*

Credible people are often "people of few words." They don't have to carry on at great lengths because their reputations precede them, and they are secure in their own value to their companies and customers.

Avoid being long-winded, especially on the phone. People don't have very long attention spans to begin with, and when they are sitting on the phone they seem to get especially fidgety if they aren't drawn into the conversation at frequent intervals.

A good rule of thumb is to spend about one half as much time as you think you should in any given conversation. Linguists report that language is inherently repetitious and that we can halve the ordinary paragraph of speech simply by eliminating wasteful words.

BEEF UP YOUR SPEECH WITH POWER WORDS

I use answering machines extensively, and I have one attached to my phone at home.

I also do celebrity impressions, and I have a repertoire of some forty voices, ranging from Jimmy Stewart to Bela Lugosi. For the fun of it, I recorded my outgoing message with the voice of John Wayne. It says something to the effect:

"Well, hello, cowboys and cowgirls. My good friends aren't available right now, but if you'll leave your name and number, I'll ask 'em to get back with you just as soon as they can. After the beep, you'll have about twenty seconds. Now here ya go! [beep]"

This recording has a funny effect upon people, and especially men who call. They start leaving their message in their own voices, and then they suddenly switch to the cadence and tone of the "ole Duke."

I believe that John Wayne's delivery is so attractive to people that they feel compelled to match his tones whenever they hear them.

I know this sounds farfetched, but I have another interesting experience to support this idea. When I was doing a large U.S. Navy training project a number of years ago, we were trying to help some of our fellow trainers to be effective with the groups with whom they would be dealing. In order to do this, we exposed them to some experienced veterans of the program who had a terrific record of success.

The best trainer sounded just like John Wayne! He kinda talked in a sorta slow way, pausing at all the wrong times, Pilgrim! He was a smash hit with the mostly male audiences with whom we were working.

I recognize that we all can't learn to do John Wayne impressions, and they wouldn't work on everyone anyway. The idea here is that there are certain basic structures of credibility in our culture that we can draw upon if we are clever, and they can help us to create bonds with our prospects on deep psychological levels.

What some of us may not be able to accomplish with *tone*, we can accomplish with *language*. Certain words contribute to sales efforts, while others can take sales away from us if we aren't careful.

Watch out for weasel words such as:

- Maybe
- If
- Could
- Might

- Possibly
- Perhaps
- Like

I'm sure you're wondering what's wrong with these everyday terms. Each one expresses in a weak manner what we should be asserting much more strongly. For instance, we might be calling someone to ask for an appointment and say, "*Maybe* I could stop by on Thursday." This is weak, as the prospect will be saying to himself, "And then again, maybe *not!*"

Let's take the same goal of setting an appointment and examine the impact of some of the other words. "*If* you have a few minutes on Thursday, I *could* stop by . . . " Who cares if you *could* stop by? *Tell me what you're going to do, you nerd!*

Let's put all of these weak-kneed words together for a star-studded illustration of a phrase that is a total abomination:

> "*Perhaps* we *could* get together *if* you *might* have a few minutes, and *possibly,* we *may* be able to see how my product *could* be of benefit, and *I'd like* to stop by tomorrow, *if* you *don't* mind."

This sentence seems as if the speaker is avoiding any affirmative statement whatsoever. To establish credibility, be sure to reduce the number of weasel words you use, while replacing them with power words. For example, instead of telling a client that you would "like to see her" on Thursday, be more assertive and say, "Thursday will be a good day for us to get together to discuss the services I've mentioned."

Notice the emphasis upon the fact that Thursday "will be" a good day to get together. I didn't say it "might be," or it "may be," or even that it "could be," but I insisted that it *will be*.

There is more at stake here than a subtle change of grammatical tense. We are altering the whole character of the interaction and the power dynamics between seller and buyer by making these small changes in our speech. We effectively take control of the conversation and our relationship with the prospect by marshaling our language choices in a meaningful and potent way.

Listen to Frank Sinatra's music if you want to hear the sound of success. There's no question he "has it." But what's the "it" that makes him so dynamic?

He's smooth, first of all. There aren't any traces of unplanned hesitation as he moves from one lyric to the next. Listen for his pauses. He puts them just where *he* wants them, and not where just any old singer would put them. When he sings about the good and bad times, you feel he's been there before, and of course, he tells his tale as if you were his closest buddy.

Sinatra doesn't simply do "show dates" or "gigs" or even "concerts." When he performs, it's an event to be remembered.

When you sell yourself over the phone, think of Old Blue Eyes and remember that each call is going to bear your own special touch.

CHAPTER THREE

THE ANATOMY OF SUCCESS: DEVELOPING PATTERNED SALES PRESENTATIONS

We have already discussed the idea that the telephone is a unique communication medium. I mentioned that telephone language differs in a number of respects from our everyday vocabulary, and that we need to be alert to different cues when we are selling by telephone.

Before getting into the structures that you can employ in a conversation, I am going to point out some significant aspects to telephone selling that will inform you how to go about the process of putting together a solid sales presentation.

CONTROLLING THE CONVERSATION IS VITAL

Most folks go about their lives without any idea as to how they can control telephone conversations. This isn't surprising when we consider the fact that most of us are generally unconscious of most of the more subtle dynamics of telecommunication.

In any case, customers are used to getting the edge on telemarketers, and this needn't be the case if we are prepared before we get on the phone, and if we listen right away for certain cues.

Here are some of the subtle things that we should become aware of:

1. *People won't help you to "save face" over the phone.* Most face-to-face selling courses emphasize the fact that potential customers like to be helpful, and if they are called upon to assist a salesperson, they will go right ahead and do it.

This sort of helping behavior is even more apparent when salespeople seem to be getting themselves into embarrassing situations. What takes place is interesting. The salesperson makes some sort of mistake in front of the prospect, and the prospect does what he or she can do to help the seller to recover composure.

In this way, the buyer can feel good about him or herself because he or she is being polite and civil, while the salesperson is spared the pain of an embarrassing moment.

Unfortunately, customers feel no need to help salespeople out over the phone. Perhaps this is because they can't see us and therefore have no sense of commitment to us, as they would have if we were in each other's presence.

Salespeople intuitively know this and feel insecure at the beginning of a call and, still worse, to discourage the prospect from rejecting them, they try to create rapport and a bond through poor techniques. For instance, an insecure salesperson will spend too much time talking about the weather or the big sports event of the day instead of getting down to business. This merely makes customers more uptight, and accelerates the rejection that the salesperson was struggling to avoid in the first place.

2. *Prospects don't regard phone calls as social situations.* They see them as interruptions of more "serious" activities. I was speaking to a prospect from a glamorous company the other day, and he wanted me to drive across town and discuss the idea of retaining my firm to design a telemarketing program.

This is a noble idea, but I am reluctant to get in the car and waste the better part of a day on the freeways and in someone's office trying to make the person feel important. The idea of making face-to-face sales presentations becomes more absurd to me as time goes on because most meetings are really exercises in procrastination and group-think, where decisions are *avoided* rather than made.

In any case, prospects enjoy meetings because they are social events through which they can show off their large desks and corner offices and other pagan symbols of power and status. This is one of the main reasons that "roadies" (field salespeople) are tolerated. Roadies enable "landlocked" prospects the opportunity to have a conversation with someone from the outside world. Even if prospects have no intention of buying, they can and will waste the time of an eager salesperson simply as their own selfish brand of occupational therapy.

What does all of this mean to the telephone salesperson? It means that unlike face-to-face meetings phone calls offer very little in terms of a "social payoff" for the prospect.

Consequently, customers won't try to prolong or assist the telephone conversation nearly as much as they would the personal chat.

This translates into *impatience*, and telemarketers have to design their messages with an eye on overall word economy, because many prospects simply won't sit still for the same drawn-out dissertation that we might launch into in their presence.

3. *Control is won or lost at the very beginning of the call.* I see the beginning of a call somewhat like the jump-ball process in basketball. At that juncture, the ball is brought to the center of the court, thrown into the air, and a representative from each team tries to get control of it by batting it to a team mate.

Conversational control is similarly up in the air at the beginning of the selling contest. What we need to do is to make sure that we get control, and there are a few tricks we can use for this purpose:

(a) Ask a friendly question. Questions arouse interest in most of us because they encourage us to speak about ourselves, which is usually pretty flattering. Make sure, though, that the question is friendly. Later in this chapter I'll mention a way of starting a call that is known as the after-mailing approach.

Poorly trained sellers turn this usually successful opener into an interrogation by putting their question this way: "Recently, I sent you a letter and I wanted to know, did you read that?"

Put in this manner, the question seems to make the customer feel he is suddenly under fire, and the result is a disgruntled prospect and the loss of a sale.

(b) When the party you want to speak to comes on the line, say the person's name with a lift in your voice, almost as if you are asking the name instead of simply stating it. For instance, I may answer the phone, "Hello, this is Gary." What I am doing is saying, "Here I am. Now, who are you, and what do you want with me?" In short, I am in control of the call because I am making you "come to me."

You should turn the tables on me by listening to me announce my name and by immediately responding, "Hello, Gary?"

I'll say, "Yes!" with enthusiasm and with an uplift in my voice, and you'll be in charge of the call because you will have made me "come to you."

Believe me, this works amazingly well, and the best part of it is its subtlety. The customer won't think you are being strategic, and this will simply strengthen the effect you produce.

(c) Beware of asking for confidential information that can threaten the prospect. I recall doing a telephone sales seminar in Cincinnati a while ago when a participant complained that she was losing control of the call at the very start of the conversation. I asked her what she was saying, and she told me she had been instructed to find out what the annual revenues were of various companies. She simply asked people flatly, "What were your annual revenues last year?" No wonder she was being rejected right and left!

I suggested she change her approach and offer the client certain forced-choice categories of response: "Would you say the annual revenues of your company are between two and ten million, or over ten million dollars?"

This was to be preferred because it actually gave the sales rep what she was after—a sound idea as to whether the prospect could afford the service she was offering. The specific dollar amount associated with annual revenues was irrelevant.

(d) Too many questions can make the listener defensive.

We can inadvertantly lose control of the conversation by asking too many questions, one after the other. Make sure to space your material in such a way as to ask for information and then in return offer information of your own to the client. This makes your conversation seem much more like a give-and-take process than an inquisition.

(e) Use open and closed questions to produce the control you need. Some sales training methods advocate the use of open-ended questions when dealing with prospects. These require more than a yes-or-no response from the prospect.

An open-ended question might be, "What are the most important things you look for in a telemarketer?" An answer has to yield information when the question has been framed in this way. Another open-ended question is, "How do you feel about the new telemarketing machines that have been coming into the market?"

A closed-ended question actually forces the customer to make a yes-or-no determination. If I wanted to engineer a particular response in short order, I might say, "Those new telemarketing machines sure are insulting to a lot of people, *aren't they*?"

Typically, prospect-centered selling uses open questions, while salesperson-centered selling uses closed ones. The closed questions give more authority and control to the seller, but they can boomerang and cause the client to feel that he or she is being forced to arrive at certain conclusions. Used properly, both open and closed questions can help us to get the information we need while giving us the control over the conversation that is justified by the circumstances.

HOW *SMOOTH* SHOULD YOUR SALES TALK BE?

When I want to relax and nearly float away, I listen to some of the "old crooners," such as Dean Martin and Frank Sinatra. I think they're terrific because they're so smooth. Every note seems effortless, and they move from one mood into the next like rows of tall grass bending in a summer breeze.

Should telemarketers strive to be as smooth in their way?

Yes and no. First of all, I would argue that a sales talk should sound natural, up to a point. It should flow without choppiness from idea to idea, and it should sound like lively conversation and not bore the listener into a stupor.

At the same time, we can sound overly smooth, whereby the customer comes to feel that he or she is being sweet-talked into an agreement. There are times when it pays to throw a monkey wrench into our delivery, in order to make ourselves sound more human and to lower the threat threshold of the prospect.

USE AUTHENTICATORS AND ASSOCIATORS

Do you remember the movie *The Great Escape*? I think it was one of the best adventure films of the 1960s, and there is an unforgettable scene in it in which Richard Attenborough's character and another British officer are about to get on a city bus and effect their escape when a sudden gaffe ends up costing them their lives.

Just as they are about to get on the bus, a German S.S. plainclothesman said to one of them, "Good luck!" The would-be escapees responded without thinking, "Thanks!" Had the Britons really been Germans, as they were posing, they wouldn't have known English, nor would they have been aware of that to which the S.S. man had been referring.

The S.S. man used what I call an *associator*. It is a term that has special personal or professional meaning for the listener and tends instantly to produce trust.

Sometimes associators are colloquial terms that aren't grammatical, yet which create the effect we want. For instance, I sometimes find myself saying something like, "Well, that was a *whole-nother* thing," instead of "that was another thing." When I use this term I am usually speaking to people who also use language very casually, and this phrase may enable me to sound like the other person and "talk his language."

Authenticators produce identification as well. What these terms do is tell the prospect that we really know our stuff. For instance, I may speak to clients in terms of "cost centers" and "profit centers," because this is the sort of jargon with which they may be familiar and comfortable.

When building our patterned sales talks we should sprinkle them with both associators and authenticators as these devices serve as cognitive shorthand for the client. They say that we are very much like them, while still being experts in our area.

WINNING WITH LINGUISTICS

When was the last time you sat down and analyzed the kinds of words you use in your sales messages? If you are a salesperson you have probably done this from time to time, while looking to insert or eliminate certain phrases that you thought were or were not really effective.

How often have you scanned your sales talks in order to detect the presence of certain specific word-sounds, such as vowels and consonants? I'll bet you haven't spent any Saturday nights doing this. Right?

Well, this is definitely an area that invites exploration. Did you know that your presentation may have too many words that start with the letter "K" in it? Or the letter "S"? Or, even the letter "H"? That's right; these sounds can inadvertently turn off clients who might otherwise decide to buy from you if you used more pleasing sounds.

Let's examine this a little more closely. Think about the *crass* sound of the letter "K." By the way, this is the same sound in the word *crass*, which I used in the last sentence. *Curt* sounding, isn't it? It almost *crunches* along as it enters our ears and our *consciousness, correct*? *Crazy*, isn't it? In fact, as I write this page, I find it nearly impossible to think of a word that sounds pleasant, if it *contains* that "K" sound.

In sum, the "K" sound is not what language theorists would call euphonious, or pleasing to the ear. *Consequently*, to the extent possible, we should avoid using it in our sales presentations.

The letter "S" can be dangerous, as well. It can sound as if it is *hissing* at us, as *snakes* do, with their *slimy, sleezy, slinking selves.* While "S's" are nearly impossible to avoid altogether, we should use them *sparingly,* and beware of *stacking several* in the *same sentence.*

"H" can be unpleasant, too. Think about ten "H" words. Here's my list:

1. Hate
2. Hellish
3. Harlot
4. Hussy
5. Horrible
6. Hornets
7. Hard
8. Hit
9. Hunger
10. Hades

I grant you that I was probably seeking nasty terms as I composed this list, but you would be amazed at the speed with which I put it together. In other words, there isn't a lack of very negative words or ideas in our language that start with a hard "H" sound.

AREN'T THERE ANY GOOD SOUNDS?

There are some sounds that are definitely euphonious. "W's" are interesting. Some of the "W" terms that come to mind right away are:

1. Well
2. Wonderful
3. Wealth
4. Welcome
5. Willing
6. Wise
7. Wishes
8. Wants
9. Winning
10. Worship

I am particularly taken with "V" sounds. Here are some of my associations with "V" words:

1. Velvet
2. Vermillion
3. Voluptuous
4. Varsity
5. Victory
6. Vanguard
7. Very
8. Valet
9. Veracity
10. Venus

That's right! Just call me on the phone and throw in the word "Venus," and I'll be putty in your hands!

"L's" are pretty nifty, too. Here's a sampling:

1. Lullaby
2. Lady
3. Large
4. Love
5. Luau
6. Laurels
7. Like
8. Lotion
9. Learn
10. Lavish

What I'm talking about here is something that poets and other wordsmiths have known for years: When you combine pleasing sounds with each other, you can produce fantastic effects.

Let's look at two brief sales talks. The first will be populated with harsh sounds, while the second will be much more soothing to the ear.

Example #1: The harsh approach
"Hello, Mr. Smith? HI, This is _____ _____ calling on behalf of the Glendale bluebirds. How's it go'in with you, today? Great.

"I'm calling to tell you about our upcoming bake sale that's going to be held at the Mark Keppel School next week.

"I sure hope you can't get enough of great chocolate chip cookies 'cause we're sure gonna have bunches of 'em to choose from.

"In order that we don't overbake, we're simply checking to make sure that a baker's dozen will be sufficient for you, or will two dozen be better?"

Something interesting occurred to me as I was putting this presentation on the page. I noticed that slang tends to be gruff sounding, while polished language flows much more smoothly. I also tried to write the script in kid-talk, which is very casual, sometimes halting, and often pretty goofy.

Note how this talk possesses a lot of hard "G" sounds, as well as harsh "H's," and hissing "S's." Let's see what we can do to reduce the frequency of these sounds and produce a better presentation.

Example #2: The pleasing approach

"Hello, Mr. Smith? This is _____ _____ with the Glendale bluebirds. How are you this (morning, afternoon, evening)? Very good.

"As you may know, our bake sale is next week, and this means that we'll have those delicious cookies that folks love so much, and we're hoping to make just the right amount so everyone will have some to enjoy, and what we're doing is providing a dozen for your family, or will two dozen be even better?"

What I've tried to do in the second talk is reduce the number of clicking sounds that make the appeal sound rough to the listener. By eliminating some of the hard "K's," I've actually been able to cut the presentation to about one half its original length.

Let's focus for a moment upon the positive "buzz-words" in the second speech. These include: *Means*, and *Hoping*, and *Love*, and *Enjoy*, and *Family*. Compare these pleasing words and their positive psychological associations with the key words in the harsh message. They include: *Great*, and *Hope*, and *Bunches*, and *Choose*, and *Checking*. I'm sure you'll agree that these terms aren't nearly as positive in their overall impact as those that are found in the second approach. In fact, some of the words are potentially complicating to the listener, such as choose and checking. These imply that the customer has to make choices, which many people would like to avoid, even if it involves a minor thing such as chocolate chip cookies.

CAPTURING THE TONE OF AN INDUSTRY

When we speak about structuring sales presentations, as we are now, we need to be aware of the fact that it isn't reasonable to expect that we can sell all kinds of people a certain product or service by using the same presentation with everybody.

It simply won't work, because people are obviously different from each other, and we need to adjust to the sensibilities of various individuals. This would seem to imply that our sales talks need to shift rather dramatically from person to person, which isn't quite true.

Here is the challenge: We need to compose our presentations in such a manner as to capture the tone or "voice" of an industry and make sure to adjust the appeal when dealing with other industries. At the same time, when we are speaking to various individuals *within* certain industries, we don't have to be concerned about changing our words as much as our tones in order to appeal to different personalities.

Let's illustrate this point by generating certain *descriptors* for two different types of businesses, airlines and banks. When we speak to executives in the airline industry we find people who sound well-*informed*, somewhat *trendy*, *energetic*, and *harried* by their struggle to keep up with a deregulated competitive environment.

Bankers are much more *calm* and *collected* and their speech reflects their *self-confidence* and the relatively *stable* nature of their field.

Given the differences in personalities in these types of organizations, I will structure my presentations in the following ways:

With airlines

- Stress new developments and new or improved features of my products and services;
- Compose the appeal with a fairly fast delivery—approximately 200 words per minute;
- Allow my voice to sound enthusiastic and very upbeat;
- Keep my language rather simple, with one- and two-syllable words, along with a sprinkling of insider jargon.

With banks

- Stress my credibility by emphasizing experience and a tradition of success;
- Compose my appeal with an average or slightly slower than average rate of delivery;
- Make my voice sound rather contained and reserved; and
- Use more refined language, employing occasional multi-syllabic terms to elevate the perception of my company as a fitting and proper firm with which to do business.

AVOIDING MISMATCHES

I was recently retained to analyze a moderately successful nationwide telemarketing firm, and I found that the folks on the phone were being instructed to use the wrong tone when speaking to prospects.

Every rep had been told to nearly shout into the mouthpiece as he or she spoke in order to sound powerful and convincing. The firm was concerned at the same time about the extremely large number of people who were hanging up on the reps without first uttering any excuse or objection. This is unusual, except when recipients of calls feel that they are being bothered.

I addressed the problem by encouraging reps to sound much more low-key, and by dramatically revising the patterned talks they were using. We found that sales went up, while the number of hang-ups diminished substantially.

BUILDING YOUR SALES TALK
THROUGH THE RIGHT ORGANIZATION

Many salespeople and others unskilled in telemarketing techniques believe they can approach the phone with a fast-and-loose style that will be more successful than using a highly organized sales talk.

They're simply kidding themselves. I have found that the very best telemarketers are provided with an expertly drafted sales talk that covers about 90 percent of the conversational contingencies that they will encounter. Each seller has before him a word-for-word text as well as answers to common questions and objections, and in having these tools, the person can feel secure that there is little that the prospect can throw at him that he isn't prepared to handle beautifully.

This enables a rep to have a difficult day emotionally, which we all have now and then, yet still sell with great efficiency. Most salespeople who don't have structured presentations sell based upon "inspiration" more than "method." Remember this: Inspiration is fleeting, while method has real staying power.

MAKING THE STRUCTURE
OF SUCCESS WORK FOR YOU

A telephone sale usually moves through four phases: (1) The Opener; (2) The Description; (3) The Close; and (4) The Confirmation. This sequence is something I refer to as The Anatomy of a Telephone Sale, and I have set forth its particulars in another book of mine, *Reach Out & Sell Someone.*

THE OPENER:
YOUR VERBAL FOOT IN THE DOOR

There are probably thousands of ways that you can begin a sales talk. I've found that thirteen openers, and various combinations of the thirteen, do the trick for me.

1. The *Thank-You* Approach

Everyone loves to be appreciated, and the thank-you approach tells a prospect or existing customer that we appreciate her business.

Here's how it sounds:

"Hello, Ms. Jones? This is Gary Goodman with Goodman Communications in California; how is everything with you, today? That's good.

"I'm calling to thank you for attending our recent telephone marketing and management seminar on the 10th, and I simply want you to know how much we appreciate your participation. . . . "

As you can imagine, this method of beginning a call will tend to make the prospect feel good about our company and us. Consequently, the person will be receptive to our appeal.

2. The *Before-Mailing* Approach

Millions of dollars are wasted on printed materials every year that bear the title "sales literature." I say this because most prospects with whom we speak will ask us for brochures and the like when they are really interested in terminating the conversation on a pleasant note and returning to their other duties.

In other words, salespeople are literally conned into sending written materials to folks who have no legitimate interest in them. I say it's time we curtailed this loss of time and money by being more prudent in determining who should and shouldn't get our goodies.

The *before-mailing* opener can help us to accomplish this while making the written materials we send out have greater impact.

"Hello, Mr. Smith? This is Gary Goodman with Goodman Communications in California; how is everything with you, today? That's good.

"I'm going to be sending some written information to you about our seminars in customer relations and telemarketing, and I wanted to check your address, quickly. I still show you at [read address]. Is that right? Well, fine.

"The information will mention some of our more ambitious consulting projects over the years, and you'll see testimonials from our clients, as well.

"By the way, you folks have about ____ people in customer service at this point, is that right? Well, fine. . . ."

From this point on, we can continue probing for information that will help us to gauge the customer's interest and qualifications for our products and services. If we find that the person really isn't a good candidate for what we have to offer, we'll save ourselves some postage, clerical time, and sales follow-up efforts by electing not to send the materials, after all. If we are speaking to a good prospect, we can highlight in advance items of particular interest that can be read in our materials before our next contact, and while we're on the line we can set an appointment or move closer to the closure of the sale.

3. The *After-Mailing* Approach

Direct-mail marketing is an excellent medium if we understand how to exploit its power. Mailing pieces, alone, seldom generate more than 1 to 2 percent response, which can make this method of selling very expensive for many and outright prohibitive for others.

When we combine the use of the phone with our mailings we increase our odds of a favorable outcome by about ten times or more. Here's why: Most of us get a lot of junk mail that we take a brief look at and then trash. We don't expect to be quizzed on the contents of what we throw away and, as a result, when we get called by the sponsor of the mailing we tend to feel slightly guilty because we "round-filed" the item. Consequently, we're more receptive to the caller, and we tend to be a little more patient, as well.

Additionally, customers take us more seriously when we have made multiple efforts to reach them, as we do when we use the mail and the telephone. When our mailing piece calls for the customer to send something back, such as a coupon or order form, this may have been considered an inconvenience that can be avoided by giving us the order while we're on the phone.

Here's how to structure the *after-mailing* opener:

> "Hello, Mr. Jennings? This is Gary Goodman with Goodman Communications in Glendale, California. How are things with you, today? That's good.

> "The reason I'm on the phone is because we recently sent out a letter and brochure, and I was wondering, do you recall seeing that, by any chance?"

The phrasing is important here because it allows the customer to scan his memory in order to recall the item. This is healthy for the sales process because he is *growing involved* with the call and comes to feel that he has an investment in finding out about what he missed.

If he does recall getting the piece, we simply proceed into the next phase of the call by reminding him of what he missed, while making sure to speak with the same enthusiasm as we would if the customer had said that he didn't receive the mailing.

4. The *New Service* Approach

This is an example of the new service approach:

> "Hello, Mr. Bell? This is Gary Goodman with Goodman Communications. How have you been lately? That's good.

> "The reason I'm calling is to tell you about a brand new customer service training course that we've developed that promises to help your order takers become order *makers.*"

It's amazing what a straightforward approach such as this can accomplish. The other day I was at home when I received a call from the proprietor of an antique shop where I have picked up a few odds and ends over the years. The woman on the line mentioned that she recalled my interest in legal bookcases and said that she had gotten one in stock that was worth looking over.

I dashed over to the store, and before I left I had purchased well over $1000 worth of interesting items, including the one she had phoned me about. It is to this businesswoman's credit that she recalled what I had told her about my interests, picked up the phone, and soon cashed in on them.

5. The *Inactive Account* Approach

Whenever I hold a seminar, I ask the participants if they believe their inactive accounts are valuable, and without exception the answer is "yes." Most of us are a little afraid of speaking to those with whom we used to do business because we think that they'll be sorry to hear from us again.

More often than not, it's the other way around. Our inactive accounts are delighted to hear from us again after finding that our replacement wasn't nearly as suitable as the client once believed.

If there is any bad blood that remains, we can try to understand its foundation and see what can be done to overcome it. It's really pretty easy because the key skill involved is listening.

"Hello, Ms. Johnson? This is Gary Goodman with Goodman Communications. How have you been???

"Well, that's good. I was looking over my records the other day and I noticed that we haven't had much of a chance to do any business lately, and I was simply wondering why this might be?"

As you guessed, this is the time to button our lips and listen. We may hear that we lost the client's business because they didn't like our salespeople, or something simply rubbed them the wrong way that they never got up the gumption to let us know about. Whatever the reason, the best thing to do is to listen politely and ask what can be done to make up for the misunderstanding, or offer a remedy of our own.

I've found that people are really very forgiving and generous when we show the courage and character to admit our shortcomings and solicit constructive criticism. The reward is usually another shot at the business.

6. The Bargain Approach

I think it's fair to say that everyone loves a bargain. It just so happens that the telephone is a terrific tool to use to introduce a bargain to a prospect because it presents a fleeting message whose opportunity lasts only briefly.

Additionally, with the phone we can pinpoint our target audience and reach a number of potential buyers with short, snappy appeals.

> "Hello, Mr. Hughes? This is Mark Smith calling on behalf of Dr. Gary Goodman, of Goodman Communications. Dr. Goodman wanted me to let you know that his *Telephone Effectiveness Newsletter* will be available for only one more week at a special discount, and given your interest in telemarketing, he didn't want you to miss this opportunity."

7. The Urgency Approach

As I continue to sell products and services, I am continually impressed by the fact that people are not likely to purchase something unless they think the item is scarce, or the opportunity to purchase is limited by time.

When you hear that something you want is on sale somewhere, what is the first question you ask? If you're like me, it's "For how long?" If it's Tuesday, and the sale lasts until Sunday, I'll probably stop by the store at the last possible moment and make my purchase. In other words, I'll procrastinate.

If salespeople fail to put a limit upon the time that an offer will be open to the public, most folks won't be motivated to spend their money. What we need to do, to the extent possible, is build a certain amount of *urgency* into our message so people won't dally about and will instead take the offer seriously and buy.

You can see this appeal in the last example pertaining to the bargain approach. I not only said that the *Telephone Effectiveness Newsletter* was marked down to a special price, but I also mentioned that this was going to be in effect for "only one more week."

What I was saying was, "You don't want to miss out, do

you?" If the sales item is attractive, a certain percentage of people will find this appeal irresistible.

8. The Marketing Study Approach

How can we qualify prospects without alienating them at the same time? How can we get away with asking a number of questions without seeming as if we are prying into matters that aren't any of our business?

These challenges are addressed very well through the use of a marketing study approach. What we do is call our prospect and say something to this effect:

> "Hello, Mr. Simpson? This is Gary Goodman with Goodman Energy Systems. How are you? That's good.

> "The reason we're on the phone is to determine how we can best meet the energy needs of folks in the community, and we have just a few quick questions to ask you.

> "First of all, do you presently have attic insulation? Is it up to the R-19 standard? And would you say that your energy bills are higher than last year or lower? And if you could be shown a way of cutting your bills by at least twenty-five percent per year, while receiving a tax credit at the same time, this would be of interest to you, right?"

These questions are obviously stacked in favor of the seller. If the questions are worded cleverly, the prospect will feel that he is selling himself, and his interest will grow as each question proceeds.

If the person isn't qualified, this will become apparent to both seller and buyer, and there will be no need to continue the relationship.

9. The Referral Approach

Few things are as persuasive in the selling game as a strong reference or testimonial. To capitalize upon the value of our present customer base we should try to get as many referrals to potential future customers as possible.

Let's say that Bob, our customer, suggested that we get in touch with his buddy, Clay, to find out if the latter could use our services, as well. Here's how we can approach the call:

"Hello, Clay? This is Gary Goodman with Goodman Communications. How're you doing this afternoon? That's good.

"The reason I'm calling is because our good friend, Bob, suggested I get in touch with you about an exciting opportunity we have in our telemarketing department. As you may know, Bob is doing very well with us, and he said that you're the kind of person who appreciates challenge and the prospect of putting his talents to work."

I have done what I can here to mention our mutual friend's name throughout my appeal because it is the strength of the referral and the trust one person has in the other that will determine whether I get the sale or not. Most folks who use a referral as an opening device deny themselves the full value of the referral by mentioning the person's name only in the beginning of the call and abandoning it thereafter.

10. The Premium Approach

When we use a premium or a giveaway, we are really priming the pump in the hope that more business will flow from our efforts. When we mention our gift at the beginning of the conversation we are more likely to arouse interest than if we wait until the end of the call.

"Hello, Ms. Avery? This is Gary Goodman with Goodman Carpet Cleaning in Glendale.

"The reason I'm calling is to let you know that we are giving away a one-room carpet cleaning to folks in the neighborhood who will ask us over to give them a free estimate for shampooing their entire home."

11. The Demonstration Approach

With the demonstration we are attempting to get folks hooked on our products and services by giving them a small taste of what we have to offer.

Restaurants do this very effectively through "2-for-1" coupons offering two dinners to folks who purchase one at the regular price.

> "Hello, Mr. Barker? This is Gary Goodman with The Goodman Diner, and the reason we're calling is to invite you and your wife to sample our new appetizers that we've just added to the menu, and, of course, if you'll be good enough to stop by next week between Monday and Thursday, we'll be happy to pick up the tab as our way of thanking you for stopping in."

12. The Special Occasion Approach

Festivity sells. On this very morning, I was jogging by my favorite park nestled in the foothills of Glendale when I saw a small crowd gathered around a brightly colored hot-air balloon. I was really tempted to abbreviate my exercise regimen to find out what all the excitement was about, and why this wonderful air machine was parked in the middle of the soccer field.

A good way of getting someone's interest piqued over the phone is to proclaim that one day or other is special and that this is going to have special meaning for your customers and your firm.

I recall one of my clients did this with an air terminal that they were opening to accommodate cargo at the Los Angeles International Airport a few years ago.

> "Hello, Mr. Shipper? This is Gary Goodman with Mega Airfreight, and we're calling to let you know that we are opening our brand new terminal facility at L.A.X. on March 28, and it promises to be an exciting new chapter in the service we are able to offer our customers."

13. The New Idea Approach

This is an example of the new idea approach:

> "Hello, Ms. Gilette? This is Gary Goodman with Goodman Communications, and the reason I'm calling is to let you know that it occurred to me that there are some interesting new ways that our training services can be of help to your firm, and I thought it worthwhile to mention some of these new ideas to you."

We place a premium upon novelty and technology in our society, and when we tell a certain segment of the community that something is new this appeal, in itself, can be very attractive. I have found that it also pays to show our hand somewhat to our prospects as I do through this approach when I say that I have some ideas that I want to share. This makes me a little vulnerable because I am really using the customer as a sounding board, and there is a chance that she could tell me that my notions are foolish or ridiculous. Customers respond well when it seems that we don't have all the answers and when we look to them for a certain amount of guidance and good judgment.

BLENDING THE OPENERS

These thirteen openers are designed so you can blend one with another to come up with just the right method of breaking the ice that applies to your needs. You can also elect to use different openers over a period of time so that you will be able to call the same client base without sounding like a tape recording of the same old appeal.

THE DESCRIPTION

The second step in your sales message is when you describe your products and services.

I have found that it pays to mention only two to four benefits at this point in the talk, because customers are impatient and have short attention spans. Moreover, people seldom buy based upon the number of benefits they perceive in something. They make their decisions more on the importance of a few benefits to their particular situation.

THE CLOSE

Closing the sale is the most important part of the entire process. This is where we engineer consent, and I have found three closes to be very effective over the phone:

The Assumptive Close

When we are assumptive, and we *assume* agreement, we place ourselves in control of the conversation and it is relatively difficult for a customer to say no, while it is unnecessary for the person to say yes.

Here's how it works. Imagine that I have already opened the conversation smoothly and have described the product, as well.

> "What we do, Mr. Jones, is set up your account with your first purchase, and in this way, you'll be able to simply charge all future orders and take as long as thirty days to pay, so I'll get this first delivery out to you on Tuesday, and we'll simply take it from there.
>
> "I still show your address as . . . "

Note that I didn't ask for consent; I assumed it. Unless the prospect says, "No, you don't," I'll continue to process the order.

The assumptive close is predicated upon the idea that it is better if we make a decision for a prospect than allow the person to make a decision for him or herself. This is the case because most people find the making of decisions very uncomfortable and prefer to defer to someone else who shows leadership. This is the function of the salesperson, who literally *leads* the person into the agreement.

There are some important reasons that I have used the phrases, "what we do," and "so I'll get," which appear in this example. These are strong ways of putting the sale into motion, and in combining my words in these ways, I avoid the devil-words and weasel-words that can destroy a close. I have covered these problems in another book, *Reach Out & Sell Someone*.

The Checkback Close

Some people find the assumptive close a little too aggressive for their tastes. A good way of softening this method is by checking back with the customer to assure that we are proceeding based upon genuine consent.

This is really easy to do, and we can accomplish it by inserting a word or two:

" . . . so I'll get this first delivery out to you on Tuesday, and we'll simply take it from there, *okay*?"

Note that I have only added one word, "Okay?" This is a very persuasive word because we are conditioned to respond positively when we hear it.

It also gives the customer a chance to decline and to offer resistance. Some sales organizations feel better about letting someone utter resistance, while others would rather not bother with it. By electing the *assumptive* or *checkback* closes you will be able to choose the approach that you are happier with.

The Choice Close

The choice close has been around for a long time, yet it is still effective. What it does is offer the prospect the choice between one thing or another, and in being asked to opt for something, it is unlikely that he or she will walk away from the conversation with nothing.

The choice close is very useful in setting appointments by phone:

"The schedule indicates a good time to stop by will be on Tuesday morning, between nine and ten, or will Wednesday be better for you?"

It becomes difficult for the prospect to decline an appointment at *some* time because we have phrased the request in the manner of a choice. If we had asked if we could come by at all, this would make it easy for the prospect to decline, altogether.

THE CONFIRMATION

When we have closed the sale on the phone, it is important to bolster the positive decision that we have generated from the customer. The way to do this is to *confirm* the understanding by:

1. Repeating the terms of the offer;
2. Congratulating the customer for a good decision;
3. Clarifying delivery or fulfillment details;

4. Allowing the buyer to ask questions;
5. Sensing the strength of commitment to the sale; and
6. Leaving the call on a positive note.

> "Fine, Mr. Jones, we'll get that out to you right away, and I show you at 631 West Broadway, Glendale, California, and do you know your zip code? Fine. Once again, the price will be only twelve hundred dollars, and that will be payable within thirty days. Are there any questions I can help you with? Okay, fine. I want to thank you for your time and your patience, and you have a great weekend, okay? Bye."

You may be wondering where I congratulated the buyer upon his wise decision. I did it immediately after he gave me his okay, and I said it with the single word, "Fine."

It is important to reinforce a positive decision right away because people can experience buyer's remorse and quickly unwind the deal, unless they are made to feel comfortable with what they have done.

HANDLING INCOMING CALLS

As I have pointed out in *Reach Out & Sell Someone*, there really aren't tremendous differences in the dynamics of incoming and outgoing telemarketing calls. In both cases, we need to lead people into buying decisions.

One of the few differences between inbound and outbound telemarketing is the fact that when the customer calls us he or she normally has a specific product or service in mind that he or she would like to know more about. Consequently, the customer has *opened* the call for us, and we don't need to duplicate this step ourselves.

Let's script a typical incoming call:

> Customer: I saw your ad in the paper for your *Telephone Effectiveness Newsletter*, and I wanted to know more about it.

That's a pretty common beginning, isn't it? We have a few choices in how we can deal with it.

One thing I can do is qualify the person's interest by asking a few questions before I deliver the information she has requested:

Telemarketer: Yes, we publish the newsletter, which is a monthly.
Are you presently selling by telephone, yourself?

Customer: No, but I supervise three other people who do, and I was wondering if it would be a useful tool for me.

Telemarketer: We have been told that managers are finding it to be the best source of new ideas in telemarketing management that they have ever come across, because . . .

Now, guess where I am going to go from here? If you think I am going to move into my *description* phase and mention two to four benefits of the newsletter, you're absolutely right!

Telemarketer: . . . it gets into who you should hire, and why it's becoming more difficult as time goes on to get good help.
It also shows you how to help your reps to avoid burnout, while you learn to take advantage of the wisdom of thousands of other people and their experiences in the field.

Okay, you are the consultant, and I'm your student: What should I do next?
If you said, "Close," you're right again.

Telemarketer: What we're doing is accepting new subscriptions at the rate of forty-nine dollars per year for the next week, and this is over fifty percent off our regular rate, so what we'll do is start yours with the November issue, and we're sure you'll find it really helpful, okay?

When we get the "yes," we simply move on to the confirmation as we would in an outbound call.

By qualifying the customer's interest and background in telemarketing, I was able to choose just the right benefits to suit her situation. This is very useful because I don't end up wasting everyone's time by emphasizing the wrong strengths of my product or service.

Another approach to the call would be to skip this qualification step and simply make two to four general benefit statements and move from there to a close. If you are in a time crunch or you have to handle a slew of incoming inquiries, this can work out even better than the qualification approach.

What happens when a customer calls and says: "I want to order your newsletter"?

> Telemarketer: Fine. The rate is only forty-nine dollars for a one-year subscription, and we'll put that on your Visa card, or will Mastercard be more convenient for you?

As you can see, we simply close the order, and then we move on to confirm it. In other words, don't stand in the way of someone who wants to buy something. Simply wrap up the call as efficiently as you can, while avoiding any statements that could confuse the buyer or make the person reconsider her decision.

In the next chapter, we'll explore how you can sell *anything* by telephone!

CHAPTER FOUR

HOW TO SELL ANY PRODUCT OR SERVICE BY PHONE

I firmly believe that we can sell any product or service by phone if we are clever and if we don't defeat ourselves before we get underway.

To illustrate this point, I have devised nine "telephone challenges," which are statements that should be considered in order to clear away the cobwebs that prevent us from using the telephone as we should.

Challenge #1: Don't say "It can't be done," because someone is probably doing it somewhere, right at this moment!
I come across people from all industries who do themselves a disservice by assuming that there are certain limitations upon the effective uses of the telephone without really looking into what is going on in other industries.

For instance, I recall doing a telemarketing and management seminar a while back, and a manager claimed that "we're going to get killed by the competition if we take our salespeople out of the field while our competitors keep theirs."

I pointed out that this isn't necessarily the case, at all. Monsanto is a good example of a firm that has opted to service distant and less profitable accounts from a telemarketing division at company headquarters in St. Louis. Monsanto has compensated for the lack of eyeball-to-eyeball visits by putting photographs of tele-reps on stationery and by setting regular telephone appointments with customers. In this way, Monsanto reps actually communicate more frequently with customers than their competitors do. (For a complete discussion of how to set telephone appointments, please see my book, *Winning by Telephone*.)

Another client of ours has found it pays handsomely to deviate from tradition and break ranks with competitors. This firm is in the hotel and motel supply field, and all of their competitors maintain large field sales units while my client does 90 percent of its selling by phone. They have found that they are the most profitable firm in their industry and their sales are growing at a rate that greatly surpasses the competition.

Don't clients miss the rapport that comes from pressing the flesh? "Not really," the executive vice-president maintains. "They perceive an actual benefit because our overhead is lower than anyone else's."

Challenge #2: Remember that selling by telephone can be a lot easier than you think.

I am amazed by the number of companies that have gotten into telemarketing by mistake and have experienced impressive success as a result. Sure, they "don't know what they're doing," but their shareholders don't know the difference. These firms are relying upon what I have termed The Law of Large Numbers, which holds that if you do enough of anything, some of it has to work out well for you. This applies to the phone because we can make so many inexpensive contacts that we can afford to "blow" a lot of them and still do enough business in order to be profitable.

Challenge #3: Sometimes one good phone call is worth more than a hundred personal visits.

Some people have less sales resistance when approached by phone than face to face. A recent study concluded that a number of people are more "persuasible" by phone because they aren't distracted by our appearance and by other environmental variables.

I have found that people who are uncomfortable speaking on the phone can actually make a faster decision through this medium because they want to get off the phone as soon as possible.

I believe that the phone also seems *more urgent*, whereas if we are sitting in someone's office it is a little harder to get the prospect off the dime and into a buying mood.

Challenge #4: The often mentioned difference between selling tangibles and intangibles is bogus.

Everything is intangible over the phone, and this is why I don't put much stock in the rhetoric I hear about the presumed differences between selling tangibles and intangibles.

If we wish to sell insurance, which is classically considered an intangible, or books, which are tangible, we would be wise to approach both efforts the same basic way.

Each item has benefits, although some are more immediate than others and some are more abstract. The key to telephone selling is to identify these benefits and make sure that they are articulated clearly to the customer.

Challenge #5: Businesses are much more similar than they are different.

I run into the claim that you can't sell two different products exactly the same way. This may be true on occasion, but I've found that it's much more accurate to say that the same principles of selling apply if you are selling fine art or fork lift trucks.

All businesses are interested in two things: (1) making money and (2) saving money. If you can demonstrate that your product or service will help a businessperson to realize either objective, you've done most of your job as a salesperson.

Most reasonable consumers are interested in comfort and value, and if our appeals are geared toward these enduring interests, we'll be in good shape.

Challenge #6: It is often easier to sell big ticket items by phone.

I recall watching a candid movie about street people some time ago that had an odd twist to it. The film showed panhandlers in New York City who asked passers-by if they could spare "some change." Not surprisingly, these tattered people met with substantial resistance, although they were pitied every now and then by kind folks who would hand over a few coins.

The producers of the film wanted to see what would happen if a very well-dressed man in a sports coat and tie asked people for "a dollar" so he could get a cup of coffee. Miraculously, people lavished money upon him, and some even insisted upon giving him more after he told them he had lost his wallet.

It seems that donors could identify much more with the clean fellow who asked for a "real sum" of money than the hobos who were really a nuisance with their petty requests. This bias in favor of the "big request" for money or action has been seen time and again as leading to the same result: Ask people for a lot, and you're more likely at least to get some than you are if you ask for a pittance to begin with. And sometimes, you will even get everything you requested.

The *Wall Street Journal* ran a very interesting article about the fact that the pricing of products is "an art," and it is often easier to sell an item at a higher price than at a lower one. Fleischmann's gin was losing ground in the marketplace when it was priced at $4.50 for a 750-millimeter bottle. When the company raised the price to $5.50 sales came up considerably over the year-earlier performance (*WSJ*: November 25, 1981).

The concept that "You get what you pay for," is deeply ingrained in us, and as a result, we equate cost with quality. This means that prospects will pay greater attention to an appeal that involves a large sum where they might reject a smaller request, out of hand.

Robert Schuller, the inspirational churchman from Garden Grove, California, points out that if we want to enlist support for our endeavors we should "start thinking bigger," because big projects inspire people to greater heights, and big people want to be associated with them.

I have tested the hunch that telemarketers would generate more respect when asking for $108 in a fundraising project compared with when they were asking for $18 to $36. In interviews with salespeople we found that prospects *actually apologized to reps when they turned down the larger sale, when they were often very rude to reps who asked for more humble contributions.*

There is nothing about the phone, *per se*, that makes it more difficult to sell a $100 item versus a $1000 item. Persuasion is still persuasion, but if we *believe* that there is some magical chemistry to the face-to-face meeting, *we'll talk ourselves out of trying to close the larger deal by phone.*

Challenge #7: Many items can be sold by phone on a one-call-close basis.

This is one of the hardest principles to get across to old-timers in the sales game who believe that selling necessarily involves a number of verbal and written exchanges with a customer.

I recall interviewing a proprietor of a small office supply company in Los Angeles a number of years ago who endorsed the idea that one had to develop meaningful relationships with customers in order to get business from them. I asked him if he thought he could sell ballpoint pens by the gross instead of by the dozen. He claimed it couldn't be done because "no one orders that way, and anyway, no one wants the pens to dry up, you know?"

As he and I were speaking, I was aware of a company three miles away that was making thousands of dollars a day selling pens by the gross on a single, cold call. What was their secret? They drove each call toward a close, and on the average, were successful in about one out of every five presentations.

I'll give you a case study of the power of a one-call-close later in this chapter as I designed it for one of my clients in the radio-paging industry.

Challenge #8: Telephone communication can be as satisfying as face-to-face communication.

Most of us foster an unconscious belief that telephone communication is inherently inferior to face-to-face communication, and as a result *we simply don't try as hard when we are on the phone.*

A good experiment to conduct is to tape record your voice as it occurs when you are looking at someone and tape a conversation with the same person as you are talking on the phone. In most cases, you'll find that your phone voice is much more inhibited and restrained. You'll also sense a greater degree of tension in your phone performance.

This needn't be the case if we concentrate upon making our voices sound *interpersonal*. This means that we should strive for vocal variety by making our volume, pitch, and rate of speech vary with the changing meanings that we wish to express. In a nutshell, inject a little *drama* into your calls and you'll find that people treat you as if you are flesh and blood instead of an alien, disembodied voice.

Challenge #9: Every phone call represents a closing opportunity.

What do customer service, pricing inquiries, and even wrong numbers have in common? They are all closing opportunities.

It must be a bureaucratic impulse that puts blinders on us and encourages us to think that people in a "sales" department should be the only ones equipped to do selling, while people in "customer service" handle questions, complaints, and operational matters.

Who said so? My company has been very successful in *cross-training*, in which we teach numbers of units how to sell in various circumstances. While most people don't consider themselves salespeople, they can still be encouraged to take the initiative to persuade customers to upgrade purchases, speak favorably of the company to others, and think positively about the firm. I treat this practice in detail in my book, *Selling Skills for the Nonsalesperson.*

We can even sell wrong numbers, if we are geared to closing effectively in all circumstances. Some of my clients reach wrong numbers, and instead of hanging up and going on to the next call, they try to sell the person they have been connected to, and they seem to close the sale a higher proportion of times this way than they do when speaking to the "right" parties. Their adreneline probably gives them the extra push that they need in these unusual circumstances.

CASE STUDIES:
THEY SAID IT COULDN'T BE DONE

I love challenges as a consultant, and I probably take on more projects for this reason than any other. In most cases, a company needs to undertake dramatic action to enhance its use of telemarketing, yet it will contend that the action that has been recommended "simply won't work" or is "impossible to accomplish."

Well, here are ten actual case studies from our files that prove we can sell anything by telephone if we are aggressive and savvy.

Case Study #1:
"Do You Really Need All of Those Field Salespeople?"

We were brought in to analyze the telemarketing procedures and objectives of a shipping company and we quickly found that we were bucking some of the challenges that were outlined earlier.

The company invested huge sums in professional sales training for its field sales staff, yet its telemarketers were virtually ignored. Actually, they were treated like clerks who had no significant contribution to make.

The first thing I noticed was the target for production that had been set for the phone reps. Each person was expected to make thirty calls per day that would result in six appointments for the field salespeople. No provision was made for closing for the sale directly by phone.

I recommended a few things. First, I maintained that the phone reps were capable of getting two "yesses" per hour. I thereby implied that they should have been reaching their targets within three working hours instead of the eight that had been allocated. Moreover, I determined that the reps should first ask for the shipment, and second, ask for an appointment if the shipment couldn't be closed by phone.

We ended up building a nationwide training program that was designed to fulfill these objectives. Our results were dramatic. Within ninety days from the completion of the project, phone reps were writing 500 shipments per month by themselves, while their appointments had shot up as well. This was astonishing to management because they were "lucky to get twenty shipments per month" in total before we undertook the training effort. The last word I got from the company was that their telephone sales unit was shooting for *5000 shipments per month* with the techniques that we had provided them, and *this goal was to be realized with no net increase in personnel!*

With these kinds of results, who needs field salespeople? This firm still believed it did, although the telemarketing force was clearly more efficient in handling new business and smaller accounts. Unfortunately, it was this sort of tradition-bound thinking that kept the company in the red, while other firms in the industry were becoming poised for economic recovery.

Nonetheless, here we saw a case where the old hands claimed a face-to-face visit was needed to earn the business, when, in fact, a well executed phone call could do the job even better.

Case Study #2:
There Is Nothing as Easy to Sell as an Appointment

In 1980 we took on a client in the advertising business from the Cleveland area that was seeking to boost the number of appointments garnered by phone through its field salespeople. Our client recognized the simple mathematics of the situation.

If their people could simply set up and see one additional prospect per day, they would have to close at least one additional deal per week. Multiply this by the dozen salespeople, and you are looking at increasing advertising revenues handsomely.

After studying the existing strategies for getting appointments, we concluded several things that we later determined were applicable universally:

1. Salespeople are unnecessarily intimidated by the appointment-setting process. There is very low risk involved in asking someone for a little time, because most of us enjoy meeting new people and being temporarily diverted from our everyday routine.

2. Salespeople think that they are "taking something away from the prospect" in asking for an appointment. How many times have you heard a salesperson say, "I'll only *take* a few minutes of your time"? No wonder they are rejected! Who wants to allow someone to "take" something from us, and especially our time, which we have been told "is money," and even more significantly, "is all we have."

3. Prospects need to feel that there will be a benefit to themselves in seeing the salesperson, even if they choose not to buy anything.

4. Salespeople regard the time of the prospect as a scarce commodity, yet they "undersell" the value of their own time. Simply listen to a salesperson mention, "I'll be in the neighborhood, so I was thinking I'd just stop by for a few minutes to discuss our line with you."

When I hear that someone will "be in the neighborhood," I am inclined to believe that the person's visit to see me is of secondary importance, and that he or she can probably stop by any old time.

This cheapens the image of the seller, who should be perceived by the client as a professional whose calendar is tight because he or she is so successful.

The answer: A universal appointment script!
"Hello, Mr./Ms. _____? This is _____ _____ with _____. How are you this _____. That's fine. The reason I'm calling is because we are the firm that [insert brief description of what you make or do], and we have developed a [insert very brief descriptive term], which has been generating quite a bit of excitement in the [insert name] industry. What I'm doing is stopping by to discuss this with folks such as yourself, and the

calendar indicates a good time to come by will be on [day] at [time], or will [day or time: pick only one or you'll confuse the prospect] be better for you?"

Before you assume that this very script won't work for you, listen to this: The advertising company that used similar "copy" that we generated experienced tremendous results. One salesman reported that his percentage of closed appointments to calls made went from about 20 percent to 80 percent! In other words, one out of five was consenting to a visit the old way, and with our methods the figure shot up to four out of five. Not too shabby, huh?

What is so magical about this script? A few things. First, as you can see, it is quite brief and to the point. We don't want to "sell the steak" over the phone; just the sizzle. When we meet the customer, we'll cook the steak on the premises.

I have also tried to use the power inherent in the seemingly vague reference to the idea that our item has "been generating quite a bit of excitement in the [blank] industry." This is known as a *bandwagon appeal*, which is quite persuasive in suggesting that "everyone is doing it, and you don't want to be left out, do you?" Most prospects don't want to be first in trying a product, but they don't want to be last, either. This appeal puts both of these concerns to rest.

"I'm stopping by to discuss this with folks such as yourself," accomplishes a few things. First, it is assumptive. Note that I say that I *am stopping by*, ready or not! I also make the other party somewhat humble by indicating that I am visiting other "folks such as yourself." This says that we "are all *just folks*," so let's be nice to each other, okay?

The real power in this script comes when we set the time of the appointment. The language at work here is truly fantastic.

"The calendar indicates a good time to come by will be . . . "

Isn't it wonderful that the calendar is dictating the appropriate time for our meeting, instead of the customer or myself? What I have done here is placed the decision on the lips of the calendar. Who can argue with Father Time, or Mother Nature?

Please note that I did not say *my* calendar indicates such and such. If I used this phraseology, I would be inviting a challenge to my authority to set the time of the proposed meeting. Instead, the calendar is set up to take the brunt of any attack, and who in his or her right mind would argue with a piece of paper?

If you prefer, instead of saying the "calendar suggests," you can substitute the words, "the schedule indicates," and you should achieve the same effect.

Remember, setting appointments is really quite simple when we use the proper approach and language.

Case Study #3:
The More You Ask For,
the Simpler You Need to Make It Sound

Salespeople make things more difficult than they need to be. One of the ways that they cause themselves grief is by complicating the selling process.

Take engineers, for instance. These people are extremely capable and are very detail oriented. They love to take things apart and put them together, and many seem happiest when talking tech, instead of good old English.

Put an engineer or a technically oriented person in charge of developing a sales talk, and you'll find phone presentations that last much too long. In fact, here is the way a typical presentation might be "built" by a sales engineer:

Opener:	30 seconds
Description:	15 minutes
Close:	Non-existent
Confirmation:	Non-existent

As you can see from this breakout, sales engineers may never get to the close because they are so busy describing the technicalities of the process or product they are hustling.

Engineers are not alone, however. The tendency to fall into this trap is quite widespread, and if we add a high price tag to what is otherwise a technical product, we will find yet another inducement for the salesperson to avoid closing: fear of hearing an objection.

I found these problems when I was invited to reconstruct a fairly successful campaign to sell precious metals. The pitch was a disaster, because it contained a descriptive portion that seemed to last forever. By the time the salesperson should have closed, the prospect knew more irrelevant details about the investment than he or she would ever care to know. I think the salespeople were really trying to assert their credibility by overtalking at this stage in the appeal.

They also believed that the price of the investment required more talk than was customary. After all, they argued, if you are trying to persuade someone to part with $10,000 for a speculative investment, hadn't you better prime the person with a gargantuan "spiel?"

Not really. People who are truly credible are usually *understated* in their approach. They encourage prospects to talk themselves into agreements, and truly "heavy hitters" learn to gracefully "meet the ball" with the bat instead of trying to pulverize it.

One of the changes I made was in reducing the length of the talk from an average of fifteen minutes to about two and one half minutes. Salespeople found that they received no more resistance from the change, and they were pleasantly surprised to find that they were able to invest their time and energy in more important matters, such as in making more phone contacts and in handling questions and objections.

When you are trying to sell an expensive item, remember to avoid making the appeal sound labored, as if you are dealing with some gravely momentous matter. Make your voice sound light and non-stressed, especially when mentioning price and payment requirements. You will be paid handsomely for making the biggest agreements sound easy and natural.

Case Study # 4:
Going for All the Marbles on Every Call

As you can tell, I am the kind of person who likes to accomplish as much as possible with every phone contact. I also like to simplify matters, and I have found that the two impulses go well together.

When I analyzed the marketing process that was being

used to sell pocket paging services I was amazed at how wasteful it was. Here is what the steps were in putting a $20-per-month rental item into a customer's hands:

1. Ads were run through various media touting the benefits of pagers;
2. Calls were generated, and the first call was handled by the receptionist who would either transfer the call to customer service, or take a message and promise a return call;
3. Customer service would take some information from the prospect and would promise a call from a salesperson;
4. The salesperson would call and set up an appointment to demonstrate the pager, and if there was interest at that point, a credit application would be taken back to the office;
5. Within three days, credit would be approved and the salesperson would call the prospect and try to set a delivery date;
6. The salesperson delivered the pager.

This process was very costly. I concluded quickly that there were too many steps between initial inquiry and the delivery of the pager. What we did was simple. We trained some inside sales reps to whom inquiries were directed. These people determined how many units were required and took credit information from the prospect. The inside sales rep also set an appointment to deliver the pager. Appointments were set up for two days later, in order to give the credit department time to verify appropriate data.

What we did was streamline the process so that inquiries could be closed on the first call. This paid off by not only saving money and human resources, but prospects tended to stop their price-shopping when they believed that their needs were going to be taken care of quickly.

Case Study # 5:
Selling the Not-So-Great Masters

You would have to agree with me that art is a very subjective subject. For instance, I find certain colors really pleasing, and purple happens to be one of them. This isn't too unusual, but you may not like purple, right?

What if I tried to sell you a purple painting over the phone? I think this would be pretty tough. Now, imagine trying to sell really trendy art items by phone, that people have never heard of, and which have price tags into the thousands of dollars. We're talking about a pretty tall order, aren't we?

We developed presentations precisely for this purpose. We broke with tradition, though, in doing it.

I find that many people who sell art are involved in emphasizing the wrong aspects of the product. They tend to concentrate upon selling beauty and other highly intangible and idiosyncratic values.

Just yesterday, I delivered a speech in Phoenix and a woman rushed up to me at a break and proclaimed that it was nearly impossible to sell art by phone because "everyone's taste is so different," and anyway, "art is a luxury item."

I stopped her in the middle of the next sentence and corrected her. "Art," I said, "shouldn't be seen as a *luxury* at all, and I think that you have just blurted out the reason for your lack of success in selling it."

She fell into the trap of believing one of the objections she hears, instead of developing a counterstrategy with which to deal with it effectively. As long as she believes that art is not a necessity, she'll use altogether the wrong appeals.

I pointed out that art should be sold, first of all, as an *investment*. Fine art has an excellent record for increasing in value. Second, I urged her to mention to her clients, who were using art to decorate their offices, that art is eminently *practical* because it makes a statement to clients about the good taste and success of its possessor. Furthermore, as I have pointed out elsewhere, beauty is practical because it inspires us toward greatness.

The woman with whom I was speaking made the mistake of defining herself as being in the "luxury business," when she should have positioned herself as being in "the success business."

When we emphasize the correct things in our appeal, we find that the barriers to selling that we have constructed no longer seem to apply. In other words, to sell art we need to concentrate upon those benefits that are attractive to people *with-*

out visual demonstration. If you remove the "taste" issue from selling art, you make this item very possible to sell by phone.

Case Study # 6:
When Friendship Gets in the Way

Sometimes we can become too friendly with our clients. A client of ours in the home building industry had to face this problem when management wanted to boost sales among its very seasoned staff.

Most of our client's sales came through dealings with contractors, who had pretty settled ideas as to the building materials they wanted to use in their structures. Our client had the formidable task of convincing prospects that they were better off using their premium product instead of a similar, though cheaper, competitor's brand.

The salespeople we were training had been with our client for an average of ten years. These were truly sales pros, who were highly disciplined and who made a point of staying in touch with contractors who had thrown business their way in the past.

While extremely friendly and knowledgeable, we found the salespeople to be overly influenced by the objections they heard. Instead of pressing for commitment, they would ease off so much as to take all of the pressure and urgency from the phone call.

What we did was teach them the language of closing and show them precisely how they were talking themselves out of deals in the misguided belief that they would be liked better by their prospects if they made it difficult for the prospect to buy. We showed them that they needed to create "emotional distance" between prospects and themselves so that they could effectively get their jobs done.

I have found time and again that we can get so close to our clients that we often avoid or forget to apply the fundamental techniques that helped us to obtain the clients in the first place.

Case Study # 7:
How to Sell Busy People

Doctors can be very hard to sell by phone because it is hard to get them on the phone, given their hectic schedules in seeing patients. Moreover, we don't create good will when we interrupt a delicate medical procedure to make a pitch for our goods and services.

How can we get through to doctors? There are two ways: (1) Speak to someone else in the office first, and (2) set up telephone appointments. Very often, doctors will appoint someone such as an office manager to initially screen salespeople and others who want something. Instead of fighting with the intermediary, we should gear our presentations to them, which will enhance their status and make them like us because we are stroking their egos. Once we have sold the office manager upon our idea, it is a much easier process to get the doctor's approval.

The second approach is to set a *telephone appointment* to speak with the head person. What we do is call the office for the express purpose of reserving a few minutes for speaking with the doctor by phone. This "appointment" is written on his or her calendar as well as our own, and it is to be accorded the respect we would show a face-to-face meeting.

Telephone appointments add dignity to the selling process. They also promise that you will have the nearly undivided attention of an otherwise impossibly busy person when he or she does get on the phone. The appointments also elevate our self-esteem because we come to see our own time as a precious commodity, while we are able to sell based upon a schedule that is mutually agreeable to prospects and ourselves.

For more detailed information about telephone appointments, see my book *Winning by Telephone*.

Case Study # 8:
Selling to Other Salespeople

A number of our clients sell through distributors, and as a result, they feel that they are in a bind. If they oversell them on particular products, ones that the distributors cannot themselves sell, they'll find that as a result they are faced with a lot of returns. At the same time, if they aren't aggressive in marketing to the distributors, the latter may find a more attractive brand or line to handle.

The tendency to be overly cautious about closing that we discussed previously definitely applies to selling distributors. I have found that manufacturers are especially cautious in trying to avoid alienating their sales agents.

What all of this does is make manufacturers and others who work with distributors *too reactive*, instead of being aggresively *pro-active*. I have found that the key to being able to motivate and sell distributors is to develop clever and exciting campaigns on an ongoing basis, in order to create excitement and involvement.

Some of this can be done through *creative packaging*. My clients have mentioned that certain distributors can never seem to buy anything other than minimal amounts of certain products, while "we know that if they stocked more, they'd sell more." In situations such as these, I have suggested repackaging various items in larger boxes.

For instance, if widgets have always come "twenty to a box," what is to prevent us from coming up with a box that holds twenty-five? I did just this in one case, and the results were fantastic. The only reason folks had sold in lots of twenty before was because "we have always done it that way."

Case Study # 9:
Putting the Prospect to Work for Us

Many people use the phone to set appointments, and some have heard that when you are on the phone you should stick to selling the appointment. Selling the product or service comes later, when you are in the prospect's presence.

This isn't necessarily true, because if we are resourceful, we can put the client to work on our behalf long before we arrive on the scene.

I have shown insurance people how to do this. It boils down to asking the prospect to do something before we arrive.

The more we can get the person to do, the more committed he or she will be to the success of our meeting.

Insurance salespeople will ask buyers to fetch their existing policies before their arrival. This can require a long visit to the bank's vault, and all the while the prospect is collecting these documents, he or she is rationalizing his or her behavior, and asking one question: "Why am I going through all of this hassle?"

The answer is: "Because you are going to save money through your new insurance policy; that's why!" In other words, by inducing the prospect to do something he or she wouldn't have done otherwise, we are making the person sell him or herself.

Case Study # 10:
System Selling

We all recognize that some sales can take weeks, months, or even years to consummate. This seems to be the case in selling computer mainframes to manufacturers, as some of our clients do.

One of the better ways to develop momentum in selling significant items such as these is through sponsoring product seminars, to which buyers and influence-agents from various firms are invited.

These programs can be aimed ostensibly at exploring trends relevant to customers and promise an informational payoff as a result. In other words, "New trends in artificial intelligence," can be the official topic under discussion, while sellers can make a solid impression and exchange business cards.

This sort of soft sell can work very well for firms that are well financed. The phone becomes more of a public relations medium, and the sale is really persuasion geared to attracting people to a free event.

When dealing with projects that require approval by many people, or which take a good deal of time to sew up, I suggest you use the phone frequently to generate mini-commitments, all of which are aimed at orchestrating agreement and keeping the deal alive in the minds of buyers.

As you can see, the phone can be used to sell anything, if we develop the right appeals and gear ourselves to getting the most from it that we can.

In the next chapter, we'll explore how we can handle some of the special challenges of telemarketing.

CHAPTER FIVE

SPECIAL CHALLENGES IN TELEMARKETING

I received a letter from a person in State College, Pennsylvania, who wishes to increase her skills in telemarketing and become a real pro. I admire her gumption and objectives, and in a sense, this chapter is dedicated to her and to anyone who is undertaking the special challenges required by modern telemarketing.

MASTERING THE MAJOR ROADBLOCKS TO SUCCESS

Anyone who wishes to prosper in telemarketing will need to face three challenges right away: (1) Phone Fear, (2) Rejection, and (3) Screening.

Phone Fear

I first discovered something I have labeled as "phone fear" fifteen years ago when I was training recruits to sell hardcover books by phone. I found something very curious about certain people. They were really outgoing when it came to meeting people face to face, and some had even had fairly successful selling careers, but when it came time to put them on the phones, their courage vanished and they froze.

I determined that what I had been observing was a special sort of shyness that was highly situational, but really potent nonetheless. Some of these folks would try a few calls and walk out with a feeble explanation about not wanting to interrupt people.

Many of us have anxiety about trying a new approach over the phone, which we overcome with a little practice and self-assurance. If you ever feel phone fear, there are two proven ways of overcoming it:

1. *Use systematic desensitization.* Systematic desensitization is a process of repeating the behavior we are afraid of in the first place. People who are afraid to meet others face to face will often join a group such as the Toastmasters in order to become gently forced into getting on their feet and sharing ideas. Over time, these speakers find that their worst fears don't materialize, and that people really find them likeable and pleasant to spend time with.

2. *Use your imagination in a positive way.* When we fear something, we often exaggerate our sense of danger. For instance, if we are walking down a dark corridor and we are afraid, every crackling noise can give us shivers. Instead of thinking about the worst possible outcome of a phone contact, we should be imagining that the prospect will be pleased to hear from us and will be willing to approve whatever we propose. It's really surprising how our own positive or negative expectations can be expressed in our voices to an impressionable prospect and be reflected right back to us in the form of acceptance or rejection.

Rejection

Perhaps the hardest thing about telemarketing from the viewpoint of the seller is the amount of rejection that he or she has to handle. I suspect there is no other field in which rejection is such a day-to-day, minute-by-minute staple of existence.

Here is the reason: Telemarketers can contact several people each hour. Let's say, for instance, that we can *contact* as many as fifteen people per hour, and make complete presentations to eight. Typically, we can hope for a 20 percent success rate, *which leaves us with an 80 percent failure rate!*

This means that 6.40 people are saying "no" per hour, while 1.60 people are saying "yes." Add this up over a calling day of six hours, and we are looking at 9.60 "yes's," and 38.40 "no's." That's one heck of a lot of rejections, right?

Simply speaking, most folks aren't trained to manage this kind of unpleasantness. As a matter of fact, I believe that *we are really trained to not handle it!* We are taught to "get along with people," and to "be agreeable," and to avoid "contradicting" those with whom we speak. In other words, there is a presumption in our early training that we really don't know what we're talking about, and if someone disagrees with us, he or she is probably right.

What happens after we hear 6.40 disagreements in an hour, and 38.40 in one working day, and this happens hour after hour, and day after day? We start to believe that our offer isn't meaningful and good, and that we're probably better off doing something else for a living.

In short, we're on the road to occupational burnout, and in the telemarking environment, this road can be very short indeed. This is why it is so important to brace ourselves against the negativity that we're going to face in terms of rejection.

Here are some tips:

1. *Don't be a perfectionist.* Perfectionists have no place in telemarketing because they can't handle the frustration that inevitably comes when they see that they are dealing with imperfect beings, and an imperfect presentation.

No appeal will arouse interest in everyone. Think about it for a minute. Imagine calling twenty people with "an offer they can't refuse." You promise them $100 for doing absolutely nothing! How much would you like to bet that half of those contacted will reject the offer, if only on the ground that "it's too good to be true?"

2. *Taking "the good with the bad" is a statistical and emotional necessity.* Don't concentrate upon the ones who say "no"; remember only the ones who say "yes." I know this may be easier said than done, but it is really important advice to follow. I'll give you a personal example from my business.

I speak all over North America and I do well at it because I am a trained public speaker and I enjoy performing before audiences. Sometimes, I'll do a very well-received presentation before hundreds of people, and the response will be magnificent, except for a disgruntled person here or there. I have to remind myself that "one monkey don't stop the show," as the old rhythm and blues song wisely said.

We shouldn't measure ourselves by our failures but by our successes, instead. If we counted rejections instead of acceptances, we would become so preoccupied with avoiding future errors that we wouldn't attempt anything at all, in order to stay on the safe side of things.

3. *Learn to view "failure" differently.* Since our schooldays many of us have been taught that receiving an "F" grade on an assignment or in a course was the end of the world and that our reputations were as well as washed up at that point.

Nothing could be further from the truth. Failure is really a very important forerunner to success, because we learn from our mistakes and are better equipped to deal with reality when it has given us a slap in the face. Purely and simply, what we define as failure is really corrective feedback that says our techniques could use a change here and there. Failure isn't a state of being that lasts forever and ever. It is a temporary condition that has to change for the better.

I read an interesting article a few weeks ago about the fellow who discovered the existence of the planet, Pluto. Instead of being an old astronomer who had been actively studying the cosmos for decades, Clyde W. Tombaugh was a 22-year-old farm boy with a high-school education who was working for the Lowell Observatory in Flagstaff, Arizona, when he spotted the celestial body. He became a sensation in the world of science, lecturing at New Mexico State University, where he was to become a professor emeritus.

Mr. Tombaugh was scanning the heavens for evidence that another planet existed when he saw one spot among 400,000 star images upon a photographic plate shift only one eighth of an inch over a period of six nights. This told him he had found the mysterious Pluto.

Imagine how many times he scoured the heavens and failed to turn up the evidence he was seeking! Undaunted, night after night, he scanned the skies in the unshakeable faith that he would detect the enigmatic planet. Finally, he was rewarded, but not until he had paid his dues by learning how to manage setbacks.

4. *Remember, they aren't rejecting you—only the message.* I believe one of the most liberating things we can do is to "role-play" various selling behaviors in order to develop sensitivity to situations as well as to become intentionally insensitive to others.

I'll give you an example. A number of women feel more secure when using a stage name or pseudonym over the phone rather than their real names because they reduce the likelihood of being hassled at home by some bozo who has gotten their phone numbers from directory assistance. Taking on a "phone name" has helped a number of people to feel less conscious of rejection because their alter-ego is doing the calling instead of themselves. In other words, it is easier for Mary Blake to handle the slings and arrows of outrageous rejection than Mary Blake Stewart, the "real" phone person.

This sort of role-playing is positive because it offers the seller role distance, or emotional insulation against the "no's" that we are all heir to when calling on the phone. I think the use of a pseudonym is appropriate as long as it is consistently used in order that clients can come to expect to deal with a certain name and not be confused.

Even if you choose to use your own name, remember that the rejection you are experiencing should not affect your positive regard for yourself. It is just a part of the game.

And Now the Eighth Wonder of the World: Getting Through Screening!

Screening can be one of the most gratifying business games around, if we know what we're doing. If we don't, and most people fit into this category, it can be a recurring nightmare each time we lift the receiver to place a business-to-business call.

The typical screening script goes as follows:

Seller: Hello, is Bill Smith there?
Screener: Who may I say is calling?
Seller: This is Bob Jones.
Screener: And what is your company, Mr. Jones?
Seller: Jones Maintenance.
Screener: And what is this regarding?
Seller: Well, I was hoping to speak with him for a minute or two.
Screener: Are you trying to sell something?
Seller: Well, no, uh, not right now; I mean if I could just talk with him for a moment he'd understand . . .
Screener: I'm sorry, Mr. Smith won't be available today.
Seller: When will he be in?
Screener: That's hard to say, but I'll be glad to take your phone number and leave him a message.
Seller: Okay . . .

No wonder we feel dejected when calls proceed like this! I am uncomfortable writing this all-too-common scenario because this kind of conversation is embarrassing for all concerned. The salesperson feels worthless because his or her attempt to make contact with a decision maker is frustrated, while the screener is forced to lie about the whereabouts of his or her boss. What a waste of everyone's time!

It really doesn't have to go this way, though. Here are some alternatives that have been proven to work better than the previous exchange.

1. Be open and cooperative with the screener. There is a successful principle of communication that all salespeople should remember: *If you want to get information, be sure to give the other party information, first.* Here is how this idea is applied over the phone:

Seller: Hello, Dr. Goodman, long distance for Bill Smith. Thank you!
Screener: I'm sorry, whom would you like?
Seller: That's okay. Dr. Gary Goodman, long distance for Bill Smith. Thank you very much!
Screener: May I tell him what this is about?

Seller: Certainly. It's regarding our recent correspondence. Thanks!

Screener: Perhaps I can help you . . .

Seller: I wish you could! But, I'm sure Mr. Smith will want to speak with me personally. Thanks again!

Screener: One moment. I'll see if he's in . . . I'll connect you now . . .

Seller: Thank you.

I'm sure you found a number of neat little twists in this approach. Let's go over them together.

a. *Use a title, to create status and formality.* I know, you don't have a doctorate degree, so it wouldn't be right to announce yourself as "doctor." Become a tree surgeon! Just kidding . . .

We are all *entitled* to use a title, if we wish, if only Ms., or Mrs., or Miss., or Mr. These can actually do a lot of good when used at the right times.

When females call males at their homes and the male's wife answers the phone, a sexual threat can be perceived by the wife if the caller states her name as "Trudy," or even "Trudy Smith." Now, if she calls herself, "Mrs. Smith," the sense of threat is either diminished substantially or doesn't even come into play.

Be experimental and see what happens when you "credential" yourself in this way. Who knows, it may confer instant respect upon your call and as a result make things a lot easier.

b. *Tell them your call is long distance.* If you are dialing a toll call of any kind, then you can label the effort "long distance." Believe it or not, even in our age of cheap long-distance dialing, people are still impressed by someone announcing a call from a faraway place.

When we do this, it is as if we are calling someone on a person-to-person basis. It is highly unusual for screeners to interfere with such expensive, first-class communications, so they put their guards down and let us through unmolested.

c. *Get used to thanking people in advance.* I forget who said it, but some sage of business etiquette once proclaimed that the two most important words we can use are "thank you." This definitely applies to mastering the screening process.

Look over the last example of screening I have provided and note how often I made a point to thank the screener. That's right. Every time I gave information or turned over control of the conversation to the screener, I thanked the person.

This does two things. It makes the person feel good about my call, and as a result, he or she is more likely to put it through than otherwise. Second, I *punctuate* the encounter by saying these words because I am, in effect, saying, "Look, hurry up and get this person on the line, because I'm through speaking to you!"

Of course, it accomplishes this politely and economically. Remember, the screener is *intuitively gauging* the importance of your call and is making a quick calculation regarding the negative impact of delaying your quest. Your politeness and calm manner will tip the balance in your favor.

d. *Don't get uppity or impatient with the screener!* Note the fact that the screener wasn't ready to receive my spontaneous "gift" of information at the beginning of the call and apologized when asking me to repeat it.

I love it when this happens, because it puts the screener on the defensive. The person has been so used to having to interrogate callers to glean information that he or she is completely disarmed when someone volunteers it.

My response was consciously cordial. I said, "That's okay," and proceeded to repeat my entire introduction, with a slightly altered phrase of appreciation, "Thank you very much!"

This tells the screener that I appreciate his or her efforts and that I am genuinely respecting the screening mission and am actively trying to help it along. This is sincerely appreciated.

e. *Validate the screener's right to request information.* When most of us are asked what our calls are about, we get defensive right away, and our indignant tone of voice asks: "What right do you have to ask *me* what I am calling for, you little *nerd!*"

No wonder things break down at this point! Do you like being belittled? Of course not, and neither do I. This is why I respond to someone's question as to whether he or she can request further information with the word, "Certainly!"

This says, "You have every right to, and I'll gladly give it." Screeners will fall in love with you if you come across this way.

f. *Treat screening as if it is a noble attempt to help your call.* It is the crowning glory of the exchange when the screener asks if he or she can "possibly help you," and you respond with the kind words, "I wish you could . . . "

This is, in effect, saying, "I like you, and I think it would really be convenient if you could help me, but I believe I'll have to speak to the party I originally requested; but, thanks, anyway."

Who can hate you for this lovely thought?

This method of handling the screening process will become second nature to you after you use it for a while. I'm sure you'll wonder why you didn't stumble upon it until now. It's really great.

Our creativity doesn't have to stop with this method, though. Here are some other ways to foil the screens:

2. *Go over their heads for a referral.* One of the main reasons we "choke" when dealing with screeners is because they treat us as if we are outsiders to the organization, and of course, we are. We don't have to sound like it, though, if we are creative.

Imagine that you are trying to reach a fairly senior person in a firm, and you know that you are going to have to deal with at least one ferocious lion at the gate. Instead of playing the proverbial lamb chop headed for certain slaughter, you can reverse roles if you like. First call the president's executive secretary. Get his or her name from the receptionist and explain that you are trying to reach the correct department. Suggest that the right one may be the one you know you should be speaking to. Very often, that person will know all the folks on board who can help you and will even mention a name or two. Note the names, and ask to be transferred to that department.

Here's how you should announce your call:

"Hello, Gary Goodman calling for Bill Smith at the request of Mr./ Madam President's [insert his or her name] office. Thank you!"

Isn't this *civilized*? If you ever wanted to hear someone leap to answer a call, this will surely be your chance. Think about it for a moment. Imagine that someone who had been referred by the president of your firm was waiting on hold for you. Would you make the person cool his or her heels? Not on your life, if you value your position.

This method is powerful for a few reasons:

a. *You are suddenly an insider.* If you are powerful enough to be hobnobbing with the president, you are suitable for the lowly functionary you are calling.

b. *You never had to say, "the president told me to call you."* All you said was you were calling at the "request" of the president's "office." The construction of this sentence is delicately arranged to make it sound as if someone urged you to call in the first place. While this meaning may be spurious, in a strict sense you are simply saying that the president's office referred you to this department.

c. *So few calls start like this that you can feel confident you'll be put right through.* Most salespeople are intimidated by the top brass in companies, so they do everything they can to avoid them. When you begin your call with the status and image of the chief executive's office on your side, who is going to try to get in your way; a secretary?

3. *Go "beneath them" to learn their secret habits.* This is another great gambit. Let's say that you need to speak to the shipping manager to deal with a person authorized to buy what you are selling, but you never seem to get through the secretary. Worse yet, he or she won't tell you when you can reach the person you are after.

Call and ask for the shipping *clerk,* instead. Rest assured that no one has been assigned to screen that person's calls! You'll get through, and the conversation will go like this:

> You: Hi, who's this? Oh, hi, Bill! Do you handle the shipping there?
> Bill: Uh, yes, but I'm not in charge. You probably want to talk to Wally Smith.
> You: Yeah, I do, but he seems to always be busy, or something. When do you think I might catch him for a minute or two?
> Bill: Gee, I don't know. Maybe first thing in the morning.
> You: You mean around seven-thirty or so?
> Bill: Or even at seven. He gets in early.
> You: Great. I'll tell you what, is he in right now?
> Bill: Hang on, I'll look . . .

And so the conversation goes. Bill is happy to tell you everything in the world about his boss's habits because:

a. Nobody ever talks to him about anything, so he's happy to have some real human contact;

b. No one has ever warned him about disclosing information to outsiders, or its risks to the company; and

c. Secretly, Bill is hostile toward his boss and hopes he gets caught by a salesperson.

You may have noticed a rather strange sentence that I brought into this approach: "I'll tell you what, is he in right now?" Isn't it a little peculiar to "tell someone" and then ask them a question immediately thereafter?

It is, but this is a terrific way of getting information while sounding as if you are giving it. English teachers may cringe at this usage, but what do they know about selling?

4. *Go around the screener to learn who is the buyer.* Sometimes screeners refuse to tell us who is in charge of a particular function in an organization, so it is up to us to do a little intelligence work of our own.

If you really want to know who is in charge of a particular job function, *call the personnel department; it's their job to know!*

Call the company, and simply say: "Personnel, please." The receptionist will think you are a job applicant, and he or she will probably be nice to you and put you through without a single question about the purpose of your call.

5. *Give the screener a "promotion."* As I mentioned earlier, we approach screeners as if they were adversaries when we should really act as if they are buddies who are just trying to be helpful.

Here is a fun way of dealing with the overly nosy screener who wants to help you him or herself:

Screener: Perhaps I can help you . . .
   Seller: I wish you could, but I'm sure Mr. Smith will want to speak with me personally.
Screener: Well, I'm pretty sure I can help you!
   Seller: Okay, fine. The first thing I need is the figure for your annual revenues last year. You probably have that "stat" handy, right?
Screener: Oh, no. Uh, you'll have to speak to Mr. Smith about that. I'll see if he's in . . .

What was the trick here? We acted as if he or she had more knowledge than he or she could have ever been reasonably expected to know. By asking an impossible question, we refuted the contention that the screener was equipped to handle the call. When shown his or her folly along this line, he or she ran for the boss, which is what we wanted all along.

FUNDRAISING BY TELEPHONE:
THE FINE ART OF ASKING FOR MONEY

I estimate that fully 20 to 30 percent of all the telemarketing in this country is being done by people who don't even consider themselves salespeople. In fact, a number of these people are unpaid volunteers who are involved in some sort of civic, community, or social development work that involves telephonic persuasion, and very often, fund-raising.

I find the fund-raising area challenging because we are asking for money without transferring any extrinsic value to the buyer. All the buyer receives, in most cases, is a feeling of satisfaction and inclusion in something greater than him or herself.

There really is an art to promoting "good causes." Specifically, there are at least three tricks involved in this craft:

1. *Don't depress the buyer.* Many non-professional fund raisers approach their work with a solemnity that sounds the death knell to a selling effort. People don't give or contribute because they are made to despair over the lot of others, but do so based upon the hope that someone else's trouble may be arrested through a gift.

I have seen numbers of telephone banks across the country where sellers are really begging instead of appealing to the right motivations. Keep it respectful but optimistic.

2. *Sound successful, already.* People like to support winners. It amazes me how much money flows into political campaigns for candidates who are "shooins" and who really don't need financing to win.

People want to contribute to causes that promise the prospect of solving the problem for which the effort exists. Success begets success, so try to make your voice sound confident and convincing relative to the merit of your offer.

3. *Use the bandwagon appeal.* Why do you think major charities recruit big-name personalities to serve on their advisory committees? They do it because we all want to associate with the famous and powerful, and feel that we're in good company when we support a cause.

Make sure to build your effort around an appeal that subtly says: "All of our friends/neighbors/colleagues are giving; so why don't you, too?"

When building your presentation, take into account some of the tips that have proven to be of value in telephone campaigns:

1. *Be specific in what you want from the buyer.* Don't leave it up to the buyer to set a figure with which he or she is comfortable in contributing. This tends to make both parties uneasy and gives the call a "haggling" feeling.

Spell out the "customary" dollar amount of a contribution, and make sure to use the closing language I have provided in prior chapters.

2. *Remember to sell two sets of benefits.* People contribute because they perceive that a third party will benefit and that they themselves will benefit through giving. Make sure to point out what the benefits are to both parties and you'll find greater acceptance of your appeal than you will if you only mention the third party beneficiaries.

3. *Ask for twice what you think people will give.* You'll be amazed at how much you can raise when you elevate your aspirations as well as the dollar amount you request during the average call. If you are hoping for $100, ask for $200. Remember, you can always accept "half."

4. *Get in the car and pick up the money.* I love an expression used by Dun & Bradstreet collection services: The sale isn't made until the money is paid."

Clever, isn't it? It's also very realistic, especially in the world of fund-raising where donors are known to make grandiose pledges that they later don't live up to because they have had time to develop second thoughts, or *buyer's remorse*.

This doesn't have to be the case, however. Designate someone to pick up the pledges within twenty-four hours. This messenger can give the contributor a receipt, and you'll find that your cash flow will be helped immensely.

5. *Before your campaign has ended, call your best contributors again.* There is a simple truism that is worth remembering: "Givers are givers." This means that if someone has already sponsored a cause, he or she is more likely to offer additional support than someone who hasn't given at all.

I recognize that you may be thinking that this will be unnerving to the kind giver. Don't believe it. If there is one thing humans can be counted on to do it is defend their past actions and rationalize their behavior by making future actions coincide with the past. Simply put, people will justify their last contribution by making another one. That is, if we provide them with the opportunity.

CASE STUDY: THE WRONG APPEAL IN COLLEGE FUND-RAISING

I really am proud of the colleges I have attended and the ones where I have taught over the years. One of my alma maters really blew it during its last fund-raising campaign, and here is how it happened.

The first thing that I noticed about the appeal used over the phone was the fact that it was really impersonal. I was told that the university was interested in erecting a few more buildings and that the overall goal of the campaign was 100 million dollars.

My first reaction, and my last as well was, "Who cares?" So what if they put up another brick and glass monstrosity with some bozo's name on the front of it? I can't relate to an inanimate object! What's it going to do *for people*?

The fact that the goal was 100 million dollars almost seemed obscene to me, for some reason. This isn't the annual budget of a number of third-world nations, for goodness sakes! Again, I couldn't relate to that aspect of the message, either.

Finally, the caller indicated that some of the proceeds would be directed at deserving students, but this didn't redeem the call because the appeal was, literally, too little, too late.

The university missed out on the single, most potent appeal it could have made to its alumni: By giving, we will make our degrees worth more by increasing the power and glory of our alma mater. Looked at this way, giving isn't an expense, it's a prudent investment! What graduate wouldn't want to know that his or her college was gaining prestige and influence, and that his or her social and professional stock would be rising in kind?

The key to using this appeal is in using some subtlety and understatement. The moral to this story is clear: If we wish to succeed in fundraising we shouldn't forget that the most successful appeal we can use is to someone's enlightened self-interest.

These are some of the special challenges presented by telemarketing. In our final chapter, we'll examine perhaps the greatest one of all: finding an answer for every objection.

CHAPTER SIX

THERE IS AN ANSWER FOR *EVERY* OBJECTION!

Do you like martial arts movies? Sometimes I find myself in the mood to rent one from a video store and pop it into the machine at home and watch a couple of overacting bozos go at each other.

Of course, I recognize that the contents depicted in these films are phony, but I still get a vicarious thrill out of seeing the good guys go after the bad guys. Justice, at the end of these flicks, always seems to prevail.

Naturally, when we are speaking to customers, we can't luxuriate in the catharsis that comes from "letting it all out," and speaking our minds, even if we are convinced that customers are throwing objections at us that are really excuses. We have to be diplomatic and professional in the way that we manage resistance and objections, and the best way of accomplishing this is through diligent preparation and guided practice.

"MODEL" APPROACHES TO MANAGING RESISTANCE AND OBJECTIONS

There are three "models" for dealing with customer flak that help us to prepare for telephonic combat:

1. Debates

I have found that folks with high school or college debating experience are excellent at dealing with objections. They are well trained for it because debators have to prepare for almost every conversational and adversarial contingency in building their arguments.

While the overall tone of a debate is openly competitive, and this shouldn't be the case in selling, debators recognize something that salespeople often forget: There is an answer for every contention that our counterpart makes, and our goal should be preparing ourselves to be equipped with the right comeback when we need it.

2. Military Training

If there is one thing the armed services are known for, it is efficient training of personnel. I was a part of the single, largest civilian U.S. Navy training project a number of years ago, where we had to train 18,000-plus people in eighteen months.

It was a tremendous experience because I had a chance to see the idea of "total preparation" in action. Our goal was to first become so adept ourselves at the training process that we could perform a number of rather complex actions without consciously thinking about what we were doing. The result was amazing. Each instructor was a marvel of efficiency and dedication, and when the going got tough, we were all able to handle it rather gracefully.

A first-class telemarketing training program should be designed on a similar basis, where answers to all likely objections are scripted carefully in advance, so that when they are hurled at us, we can handle them routinely and not panic at the first sign of a client attack.

3. Non-Violent Retaliation

Perhaps the best way of viewing the process of answering objections and meeting resistance is by thinking of responding nonviolently and nonemotionally. There are even some martial arts that are geared to being less punishing than others.

Judo, for instance, attempts to use the momentum of an opponent's thrust against the attacker by destabilizing the person, instead of trying to meet the attack with equal and opposite force.

This will be our approach when deflecting interruptions that occur when we are in the beginning or middle of our appeals.

Before looking into some of the ways that we can prepare our responses, we should examine our marketing posture to determine our strengths and weaknesses.

WHERE ARE YOU MOST VULNERABLE?

If we wanted to devise a security system to protect our homes or offices, what would we do first? We would assess our strengths and liabilities and pretend that we were burglers. Now, where would we enter the premises? What are the most glaring and inviting deficiencies in the structure? Where can we break in?

To foil would-be burglers, we need to go through this mental exercise, and to be well-equipped telemarketers we should perform a similar *vulnerability survey*. Ask yourself these questions:

1. *What is the weakest point in my presentation?* The Opener? Description? Close? Confirmation?

When you have determined what it is, you should revise your presentation to deny the prospect the ability to break in at that moment.

I'll give you an example of a script that invites interruptions. See if you can detect the points of vulnerability:

"Hello, Mr. Jones? This is Gary Goodman with Goodman Communications in Glendale, California. I'm not interrupting anything, am I?" [*"Of course you are, nerd; now spit it out—what do you want?*]

"Well, the reason I'm calling is because we sent you a letter and brochure and we're just checking to see if you got it . . . " [*"I can't remember. I throw most of that stuff out."*]

"Oh. Well, it would have told you about our special offer on the *Telephone Effectiveness Newsletter* . . . " [*"Oh, yeah, I may have gotten that, but I'm not interested."*]

This is a painful example of a script that *invites* its own termination. Recapping the many points of vulnerability, we can see these problems:

a. Never ask a client if he or she is busy or try to confirm that you have not interrupted the person's life. This is a classical opportunity to be put down, right back into the telephone's cradle.
   If a prospect is too busy to carry on a conversation with us, he or she will let us know very quickly.

b. Don't tell a prospect you are *"just* checking to see if you got it," or *just* calling for one reason or other if you are hoping to accomplish something other than dealing with that one item. If a client hears that your agenda for the call is limited to one or two items, he or she will hold you to your word and insist upon going on to other things when he or she believes your talk should be finished.

c. Don't give a prospect a partial and insufficient explanation that leads to nowhere, as this vignette did when it said, "It would have told you about our special offer on the *Telephone Effectiveness Newsletter* . . . "
   What can the prospect be thinking at this point? "So what?" Remember, don't throw the ball to the prospect when he or she can end the game by sitting on it. Keep control until you have told enough of your story so the buyer can make a reasonable purchasing decision.

2. Another question you should ask as a part of your *vulnerability survey* is, "What are my weakest appeals?" Prospects don't want to wade through a sea of irrelevant features and benefits with us, so we need to distill our presentations in a way that is consistent with my suggestions in Chapter Three. Mention no more than four benefits during any particular presentation, and remember, those items that seem most attractive to you about your product or service may generate a "ho-hum" reaction from the listener. When you find buyers interrupting you over several calls at the same point in your talk, and it happens to follow your discussion of a particular appeal in each instance, *jettison the appeal and fashion a more appropriate one.*

3. Ask yourself, "What are the weakest aspects of my offer?" Here is where we find resistance based upon pricing, timing of the offer, pressure from the competition, or based upon indifference. These reactions comprise the essential objections that we will need to be prepared to handle on the spot.

Let's examine them in detail, and generate some workable comebacks:

Price

When I ask my clients to name the objection that gives them more of a challenge than any other, the most common one I hear is "price." It seems that all of us who are involved in selling would love to run and hide from this one because it is pretty tough to handle if we can't offer discounts and satisfy the bargain hunters we are trying to persuade.

There are some very good ways to handle a "money" objection such as this:

a. *"You get what you pay for."* This is a truism in our society, and all of us have had experiences when we have purchased cut-rate products that have had to be replaced because they weren't bargains at all.

As a matter of fact, as I write these words, there is a painter at work redoing my conference room where one of his less expensive predecessors had botched the job. I will end up paying one and one half times the premium rate for the job because I tried to get away with paying half price to begin with.

b. *"We're not for everybody!"* When I think of this appeal I think of the character Sir John Gielgud plays in so many films where he affects a stuffy manner. What we are doing when defending our price or fees based upon *exclusivity* is really appealing to someone's snobbish nature and inflated self-concept.

It *does* work with some clients. How many pair of designer jeans do you have in your closet or drawers? Oh, come on, tell the truth! I'll bet you have purchased something with a "designer" name on it within the last eighteen months; am I right? I know I have. Why do we do these things? For two reasons: (1)

we like products with high social status; and (2) we foster a belief in brand names.

Our clients, on the whole, are motivated based upon these things, too, and we can use this to advantage.

c. *"You can afford it, and you deserve the very best!"* Chivas Regal makes a big deal over the fact that it is a relatively expensive Scotch, and this appeals to a lot of people who look at ordering a drink as a special reward and method of self-indulgence. "And, anyway," their thinking goes, "I can afford it."

d. *"This isn't an expense—it's an investment."* If we are selling items to businesses, they are interested in bottom-line profits, and if we can demonstrate that there is a pay-back of their investment with us, they'll come to regard the transaction as less of a burden.

e. *"It only costs pennies a day . . . "* How many dish-washing commercials can you remember that have used some variant of this appeal? Plenty, I assure you, because it offers the buyer an *important justification* for purchasing. If we must look at the purchase as an expense, it is better to take the sting out of it by pointing to the years of trouble-free use someone will derive from it, and so forth.

f. *"You're paying for service as well . . . "* I heard this answer just today, when I was speaking to my stockbroker, Scott. I mentioned that I was having a difficult time rationalizing the idea of keeping one of my accounts with his firm when I could literally halve the commissions I pay by dealing with a "discounter."

He handled me very well, although unpersuasively. He said he couldn't blame me for being concerned because we were dealing with a pretty dramatic difference in commissions. "But," he pointed out, "I know you need intelligence about various industries in order to make proper buying decisions, and another thing you have to be concerned with is whether that kind of firm can provide you with timely executions of your trades."

He got me thinking! "Gee," I was wondering, "how many trades would it take for this no-name firm to blow for me to really be handing back to them all of the "savings" they are going to give me?"

I'm still thinking . . . good job, Scott!

Timing

Customers are constantly trying to put off salespeople with various timing excuses, such as: "We're too busy now to deal with that," or "I have no time to talk with you," or "We're not ready to make a change yet."

Sometimes, these excuses are accurate, and other times we can recognize that they are "fabricated from whole cloth." What can we do about them?

One of the best ways to handle this excuse is to take it away from the prospect to begin with. Here's how. Build *urgency* into your message. For instance, limited-time offers are excellent because they will self-destruct on a given day, and customers recognize that they'll have to make fast decisions or else miss the opportunity.

Whenever you sell, try to *structure time* in this fashion for the prospect. Another way of looking at this process is by calling it *track selling*. Track selling puts the marketing flow on a calendar, where both salesperson and prospect have agreed that certain events should take place at certain times. When you are selling complex opportunities or products, this kind of salesperson/prospect cooperation can really be helpful in keeping things moving along smoothly.

Competitive Pressure

How do you feel when a prospect tells you that he or she is dealing with your competitors? Warm and tingly? Not me. My first impulse is to blurt out:

> "How can you do that, you *bozo*? Dealing with Abba Zabba Telemarketing is the most *bozaic* thing you could ever do! Do you have any idea about the background of those *nimnoids*? They used to sell light bulbs and now they think they could teach brain surgery if you gave them an outline!

108

"My opinion of you, Mr./Ms. Prospect, has just taken a dive to the depths of the Grand Canyon!"

This is what we might love to say, but you can well imagine the response we'd get in return. Instead of doing what our "gut" tells us, as in this case, we should use this objection as a way of:

1. Learning about the strengths and weaknesses of our competition; and
2. Causing the client to *comfortably reconsider* the wisdom of continuing to employ those buffoons!

When the client says, "We're using Abba Zabba, and we're pleased as punch with them," say:

"That's fine, Mr./Ms. Prospect. What do you like most about them?"

This conciliatory and open-ended question will make the customer feel that it is safe to tell you about your competitor, and while he or she is doing so, you will be getting an inside glimpse of that party's effectiveness and methodology.

The next question to ask is: "And if you were going to do anything to improve their product or service, what would it be?" This will tell you where your competitor is vulnerable and you can thereafter formulate an appeal that exploits his or her weaknesses and promises relief to the client who is suffering for one reason or other.

Where you sense that there is a closed door and there is such complete satisfaction with the present supplier that you don't have any chance at all, don't give up. Ask one final question:

"What would it take to earn your business?"

Often, this line will shake the customer up so that he or she will see that you are seriously interested in doing business. Sometimes, this is all it takes to create a small opportunity that will help you to break through a competitor's barrier.

One of the more common interruptions that we hear is the comment, "I'm not interested." This message is often uttered toward the very beginning of the talk, when the customer hasn't heard enough in order actually to become interested.

I have found that this objection is best answered by using a device that will enable us to continue our planned talk, which is really geared to the goal of creating interest. The device that I have found to work very well is the *transition phrase*, which I discuss in some detail in *Reach Out and Sell Someone*.

What the transition phrase does is agree with the prospect, thus creating a telephone climate that will enable us to continue with our presentation. One such phrase is, "Well, I understand that, but . . . "

What we should do is read our presentation in such a way as to make it sound as if we aren't going to be interrupted at all. When the prospect says, "I'm not interested," we should listen to this comment, and then in a pleasing voice, say "Well, I understand that, but . . . " and go right back to the presentation where we left off.

You'll be amazed at how well this works, and how smooth it sounds "in reality." For other transition phrases and pointers on how they can be used to control conversations see both *Winning by Telephone* and *Reach Out & Sell Someone*.

When you hear this objection claiming disinterest and you have completed the main body of your talk, it is usually a signal that you have used the wrong benefits and you should probe at that time to find out what really appeals to the buyer.

I have found that the use of a bottom-line question can work well:

"If I can show you how to [insert benefit], this would be of interest to you, right?"

If there is any hope for getting a sale, this sort of *no-bull question* will ferret it out for you.

110

Prospects can become emotionally unhinged as any of us can. We should be prepared to handle the irate or difficult client because there can be gold waiting for us if we show maturity and manage the emotional moment properly.

One of the things that can send a customer into orbit is when we stumble upon a message that he or she can take defensively. Here are some of the messages we should avoid that cause *defensiveness*:

1. *Evaluation:* Watch out for using phrases that can sound as if you are negatively evaluating some action of the client. For instance, you don't want to say, "You shouldn't have done that," or "That move was certainly foolish."

2. *Control:* I have encouraged you to try to control the conversation and be assumptive at various times. This is valuable, but make sure not to let the client come to feel that he or she is being railroaded into a decision. Develop your talk in such a way as to give the other person the feeling that he or she is participating actively in it.

3. *Strategy:* Clients get uptight when they think we are keeping certain information from them. Try to sound open and spontaneous at all times.

4. *Neutrality:* Avoid taking on the manner of total, clinical objectivity because it is alienating to most of us. Express yourself and air some of your own feelings from time to time. This will make you seem like flesh and blood and it will be appreciated.

5. *Superiority:* People don't like to be made to feel inferior. They'll do almost anything to show us "you're not so great" if they feel that they are being treated in such a manner. Deal with prospects as equals.

6. *Certainty:* You may really know your stuff but you don't want to come across as being infallible. If you seem as if you're "perfect," people will find your feet of clay and smash them.

Avoid phrases such as: "You'll have to," and "There's no other way," and the like. When we hear these claims, our first impulse is to dispute them.

WHEN YOU MAY *NOT* WANT TO ANSWER AN OBJECTION

Although every objection may be answered, you may find that there are some that you will want to accept, either as a matter of policy or economy.

For instance, when I am associated with companies that phone consumers at home, I recommend that they require telemarketers to believe people who say that they are unemployed or experiencing difficult times. I look at it this way: There are enough people who *are* equipped financially to manage the money involved in the offer, so why not call them?

Additionally, I think it is dehumanizing to put pressure upon people who aren't solvent. It really doesn't accomplish anything, except to upset both the caller and the prospect.

I don't believe it is worth wasting time on people who seem to be challenges, either. You know the ones—people whom we have never sold, the really hard-bitten ones. Instead of marking imaginary notches on our phones like the gunslingers of old would do when felling an adversary, we should be more interested in hunting for the scent of a truly *bona fide* qualified customer. Remember, we're not in business to count challenges, but dollars that result from sales. So why not accept the easy ones that come along, every now and then?

PRACTICE YOUR DELIVERY

All great professionals practice. I am amazed that the best baseball players in the world congregate in spring training to go over the basics of their discipline: hitting, fielding and baserunning.

These pros know how to do these things better than anyone else on earth, so why should they bother practicing? Because they, above all others, recognize that true winners are the ones who execute the ordinary, exceptionally well. Professionals are, ultimately, the best detail people around.

Practice the timing of your answers to objections. Try to make your comebacks to interruptions sound effortless, while making your overall presentations sound smooth and seamless.

When you have accomplished this, you'll know that *You Can Sell Anything by Telephone!*

AFTERWORD

Thank you for reading my book. I enjoyed writing it, and I hope you will profit greatly from using it in your day-to-day business.

Throughout this book, I have mentioned my other books, *Winning by Telephone*, *Reach Out & Sell Someone*, and *Selling Skills for the Nonsalesperson*. You're probably wondering if they are sufficiently different from *You Can Sell Anything by Telephone!* to warrant your attention.

I can assure you that they are, and I can recommend them strongly because thousands of readers such as yourself have made them best sellers.

The key to any idea or book is to be found in its ultimate usefulness. I would like to hear your reactions to the information you have found useful in this book, and I invite you to write to me at the address I have provided below.

If you would like to hear of our training seminars in telemarketing and management, customer relations, and in selling skills, please let me know. We also publish a complete line of training tapes as well as the *Telephone Effectiveness Newsletter*, a monthly subscription publication.

I wish you the very best.

Gary S. Goodman, Ph.D., president

Goodman Communications Corporation
P.O. Box 9733
Glendale, California 91206
(818) 243–7338

INDEX

118